The year of 1968 was one of exceptional political significance in the United

States. Its significance was largely based on the fact that the contest for the presidency

and for seats in Congress had a profound effect upon the course of the war in Vietnam. A

brief background of the Vietnam policy affected by these contests follows.

Early in February of 1965, Lyndon Johnson undertook a major escalation of

United States involvement in the war in Vietnam, by beginning the bombing of North

Vietnam. At that time the struggle for control of South Vietnam was primarily a civil

war waged between rival groups under the rival banners of the Saigon Government and

the National Liberation Front, and the Saigon Government was gradually losing. United

States military assistance to the Saigon Government then exceeded North Vietnamese

assistance to the NLF.

The bombing of North Vietnam was presented to the American people by the

Johnson Administration as a limited response to North Vietnamese aggression. John T.

Butchko graduated from Glendale High School in June of 1955. He had received all "A"

grades throughout high school, except for some classes in physical education, and he

finished first in his class. He attended the University of Southern California and the

University of Southern California School of Law. While attending the University of

Southern California before going to law school, Butchko received all "A" grades, outside

of some classes in physical education.

Butchko sought high grades in law school and he generally achieved them.

When he graduated from law school in 1962, his final class standing was second in a

class of 113 students. He just missed being first in his class by a fraction of a percentage

1

point. In 1961 and 1962, he was an associate editor of the Southern California Law Review. His favorite activities during law school years were playing chess and bridge and talking for hours with fellow students between classes in the comfortable law school lounge. When Butchko attended USC Law School, it was as good as any law school in the country because of its faculty. In high school, college, and law school, Butchko was considered a liberal Democrat.

After graduating from law school, he passed the California Bar Examination, and worked as a law clerk for Judge William M. Byrne, Senior, of the United States District Court for the Southern District of California from September of 1962 into September of 1963. When Butchko was working as a law clerk for United States District Judge William M. Byrne Sr., Judge Byrne told his court clerk that Butchko was the best law clerk he ever had. While Butchko was working as a law clerk for United States District Judge William M. Byrne, Sr., he attended night graduate classes at the University Of Southern California School Of Law to earn a Master of Laws Degree. The Master of Laws Degree was awarded to Butchko in January of 1964, while he was working as an associate in the law firm of Richards, Watson and Hemmerling after Butchko completed a course in legal writing, which he worked on during weekends.

In September of 1963, Butchko took a job with the prestigious downtown law firm of Richards, Watson and Hemmerling. Richard Richards, the leading partner in the law firm for which Butchko worked, had previously been a Chairman of the Los Angeles County Democratic Central Committee and twice the Democratic nominee for United States Senate from California, and twice California State Senator representing all of Los Angeles County. Richards was a liberal. When Butchko worked there his name appeared on the letterhead of all of the stationery of the firm of Richards, Watson and Hemmerling. When Butchko left the firm, Glen Watson told Butchko that at the kind of work he did, Butchko was the most efficient associate the firm ever had.

Butchko worked in the Richards firm, into July of 1965. He then took a job in another downtown Los Angeles law firm. He stayed there only until the end of 1965, but long enough to add enough capital to his earlier savings to enable him to plan and begin his political move.

Butchko attended the Christmas party of the University of Southern California Law School Alumni Association in December of 1965. At this party, Dorothy Nelson told Butchko that she had heard that he had done good work in the Hemmerling firm (meaning Richards, Watson and Hemmerling).

In January of 1966, Butchko changed his residence from Glendale to Burbank in the Twenty-Seventh Congressional District. He was twenty-eight years old. His decision to move in that direction was based entirely on the fact that the Twenty-Seventh Congressional District had a Democratic registration of 60% and was represented by a Republican Congressman named Ed Reinecke. At that time he knew nothing about the politics of the District except that Everett Burkhalter had once defeated an incumbent Congressman, Edgar Hiestand, using the latter's affiliations with the John Birch Society as a major issue. Butchko did not plan to run in 1966 since he felt that a race for Congress should be preceded by at least a year and preferably two years of political activities in the district.

In January of 1966, he rented his office in the "Civic Center Building" on Olive Avenue in downtown Burbank and across the street from the Burbank Courthouse.

He was doing business in February of 1966, and an article was published in the Burbank Daily Review in February of 1966 describing the opening of Butchko's law office and describing his educational and professional background. Butchko put his signed Master of Laws Degree on his wall in his law office in Burbank.

The Twenty-Seventh Congressional District of California then consisted of the entire northern portion of Los Angeles County including the high desert area of the Antelope Valley, Lancaster and Palmdale; the Newhall-Saugus and adjoining Canyon areas; and certain suburban areas of Los Angeles, including Sunland and Tujunga, North Hollywood, the eastern portion of Van Nuys, Panorama City and a large portion of the City of Burbank as well as Sun Valley. The North Hollywood, Sun Valley, Panorama City, and Van Nuys portions of the district were located in the Forty-Second Assembly District, where registered Democrats heavily outnumbered registered Republicans and where Robert Morsetti, a conservative Democrat held the Assembly seat with the blessings of Jess Unruh, Speaker of the Assembly and a power politician with ambitions of moving up.

The remaining areas of the Congressional District were located in the Sixty-Second Assembly District. The Sixty-Second Assembly District had a majority of registered Democrats, but the margin there was smaller, and the area had a more Republican voting history than the Forty-Second. The Sixty-Second was in 1966 represented by Republican Assemblyman Newton Russell, who was regarded by the liberal Democratic activists in the area as a Jess Unruh Republican, and who could be counted on to give key Assembly notes as requested by the powerful Democratic Speaker. In return for his votes, Mr. Russell could expect that Jess would not give

4

notable financial assistance to any Democratic challenger, for his seat. In view of this understanding, Mr. Russell's seat seemed secure for the conservative newspapers in the district would support him over a Democrat.

The total registration in the Twenty-Seventh District was approximately 60% Democratic at the time of the June 1966 primary. The Democratic percentage dropped to about 58% by the time of the November general election. The district always had a particularly interesting political history. In 1961, the Democratic controlled state legislature had drawn the district boundary lines in such a way as to enable a popular conservative Democrat, Everett Burkhalter, to unseat Republican Congressman Edgar Hiestand, a known member of the ultra-right wing John Birch Society. Burkhalter's years spent on the Los Angeles City Council and as an Assemblyman had given him wide exposure. Burkhalter was opposed in the primary by a California Democratic Council endorsed candidate named Chuck Moses. Burkhalter won the Democratic nomination. Burkhalter won in 1962, using the alleged extremism of his Republican opponent as the primary issue. Giving illness as the reason, the elderly Burkhalter did not seek re-election in 1964.

While Lyndon Johnson swept the nation and California in 1964, the Congressional seat in the Twenty-Seventh was taken by a Republican, Ed Reinecke, in a stunning upset. Tome Bane, a Democratic Assemblyman for the Forty-Second Assembly District, sought the Congressional seat with every expectation of an easy victory. But Mr. Bane succeeded in antagonizing the literal activists in the District, who were largely grouped in the California Democratic Council, a statewide federation of democratically organized clubs consisting of grass roots party workers, many of whom tended to profess liberally oriented political principles. The activists in the clubs put whatever pressure they could on party office seekers to conform to these principles, or at least to some principles. Their most effective method for exerting pressure was the club's procedure for pre-primary endorsements of candidates. This kind of pressure had proved an irritant to opportunistic office seekers so that there was quite generally a friction between local clubs and Democratic office seekers. In many districts, rival clubs dominated by Jess Unruh and by local party office holders aligned with him opposed in every way they could the efforts of the California Democratic Council club leaders to increase their political standing in the district and on County Central Committees and on the State Central Committee.

In the Twenty-Seventh Congressional District, this friction came to a head when Tom Bane, told the California Democratic Council clubs he would win without them in 1964. Bane was closely aligned with Jess Unruh; the California Democratic Council clubs did not endorse a candidate for Congress in the 1964 primary. Mr. Bane won that primary by a large margin over Dallas Williams, a Burbank City Councilman with a significant personal following. Some California Democratic Council club members actively sought to defeat Tom Bane in his general election contest against Reinecke. These efforts included telephone messages to registered Democrats asking them to vote against Bane.

Mr. Reinecke did not appear to be a particularly awe-inspiring candidate. He had lived in Southern California since early childhood. He had taken an engineering degree at the California Institute of Technology. His father's lawn sprinkler manufacturing firm in the San Fernando Valley provided Mr. Reinecke with an income

6

and a position of corporate vice president. Reinecke joined a large number of service clubs and some veteran's organizations in the San Fernando Valley area preliminary to launching his political career.

By 1964 he had obtained some public exposure and some knowledge of the conservative power centers in the Sixty-Second Assembly District. He had acquired a leadership position in the Kiwanis Clubs.

Reinecke now moved in a circle of well-held and socially significant friends. Republican Party leaders recognized that this good-looking engineer in his early forties presented an image, which could be packaged and sold to a broad section of voters.

Reinecke had taken care to cultivate and win the support of the ideology oriented right wing political activists and party backers. These were frequently members of the John Birch Society as well as hard working Republicans. The Birch Society had a larger following in the conservative Sixty Second Assembly District than in most places, and Birch Society leader Edgar Hiestand, had even carried the nominally Democratic Sixty-Second Assembly District in his losing Congressional race with Burkhalter.

It was rumored that Reinecke was Hiestand's handpicked candidate for 1964. In any event, Reinecke was able to get Hiestand to support him.

Reinecke won the GOP Congressional nomination in a close primary contest with William P. Gale, a retired Army Colonel and resident of Saugus. Gale was an ultraconservative. After winning the primary, Reinecke campaigned hard against Bane. He visited industrial plants and shook hands with workers. He personally campaigned in markets and stores and displayed great appeal to women voters of all ages.

His public relations manager, Bob McGee arranged localized publicity, newspaper advertisements, and spot radio advertisements. Reinecke was presented in publicity as an eligible bachelor. Reinecke was divorced and had not remarried.

Bane did not campaign nearly as hard, and he was seldom seen in the Sixty-Second Assembly District. Bane was embarrassed by a Reinecke disclosure that a business associate of Bane's was conducting a pornography enterprise in the San Fernando Valley. Reinecke arranged to be photographed while he appeared to personally uncover the smut in a warehouse. Bane was Jewish, while Reinecke was a member of a Lutheran Church.

The final vote was 83,141 for Reinecke to 77,587 for Bane in a district who's registered Democrats were more than 61% of the total registration.

The 1966 elections presented the first opportunity for the votes to indicate some reaction on the policy of escalation and continuation of United States military involvement in Vietnam.

Republicans gained seats in Congress and they gained governorships. During the years of the war in Vietnam, Butchko frequently discussed his opposition to that war in conversations with his father at his father's house in Glendale.

In 1966, most establishment politicians of both parties supported the war policies of the Johnson Administration. Many politicians of the right favored more escalation. A few Congressmen and Senators indicated their disapproval of the policy of escalation. Notable among these were Senators Fulbright, Morse, McGovern and Gruening. Congressman George E. Brown, Jr., from the Twenty-Third Congressional

District of California was an early and consistent opponent of the war policies of the Johnson Administration.

Johnson said he was glad that the peace candidates were defeated in the 1966 primaries.

In the spring of 1966, Governor Brown of California used his power and influence to get the California Democratic Council to remove its President, Simon Cassady, at its annual convention in Bakersfield. Governor Brown clearly did this because of Cassady's outspoken criticism of the war in Vietnam.

In California, Governor Edmund G. Brown gave nominal support to the Vietnam War policies of the Johnson Administration. His re-election bid was defeated by Ronald Reagan, a Republican, running with the endorsement of the powerful Los Angeles Times. Reagan had stated during the course of the campaign that he favored turning Vietnam into a parking lot. It was a favorite strategy of right wing politicians both in 1966 and in subsequent years to claim that the war could be concluded by a more complete escalation.

Political trends throughout the nation were reflected in the highly interesting Twenty-Seventh Congressional District of California.

In January and February of 1966, Butchko attended several meetings of the Burbank Democratic club where he walked right into a significant episode of the political history of the Twenty-Seventh District. Arthur Carstens, an elderly labor professor at the University of California at Los Angeles, was campaigning for the Democratic nomination for Congress in the Twenty-Seventh District. John A. Howard, a young attorney, already officing in the same building as Butchko, was also planning to run. Carstens was running as an avowed peace candidate at a time when it was commonly believed that peace candidates could not win elections. Butchko felt that the war in Vietnam should be de-escalated and ended as soon as possible. His sympathizers were with Carstens as soon as he heard Carstens speak at a meeting of the Burbank Democratic Club. He declined Howard's request to support the latter since Howard said that he supported the Vietnam policies of the Johnson Administration.

In April of 1966, an article in the Burbank Daily Review stated that Butchko was serving on the Law Day Committee of the Burbank Bar Association.

While he was working to build his practice in the first part of 1966, Butchko worked in the Carstens campaign largely under the supervision of Jeanne Caya, who has been the mainstay of the Burbank Democratic Club for many years and a veteran of many years of fighting with anti-California Democratic Council groups in the district. Butchko walked his precinct on behalf of Carstens, and it was one of the few precincts in Burbank, which Carstens carried in the primary.

During this primary campaign, Butchko had an opportunity to survey and learn by experience the important factors in the politics of the district.

Howard was supported in the primary by Eugene Radding, a law partner of Richard Rogan. Mr. Rogan was for many years the most prominent attorney in Burbank. He had been Chief Deputy Attorney General of California during part of the administration of Governor Brown. Both Rogan and Radding were among Howard's campaign contributors in the primary. Howard also got assistance from Carmen Warschaw, a Democrat with purse strings and a friend of Jess Unruh and Mayor Sam Yorty. Howard felt he had no chance to get the California Democratic Council endorsement, and so he did not appear at the local endorsing convention. The California Democratic Council clubs endorsed Carstens at their district convention. The Machinists Union and the County Federation of Labor, AFLCIO, endorsed Howard.

Both Butchko and Howard were Catholics. In those days Catholics were not permitted by their Church to join the Masons.

In Howard's mailer, used in the primary campaign, Howard stated that the United States could not leave Vietnam until the aggressors are defeated. Jess Unruh was supporting Howard over Carstens during the primary campaign.

In those years and through 1972, the California Bar Examination was regarded as the most difficult in the United States, and being an attorney in California, carried much prestige, added to a candidate's image and was a very favorable ballot designation. There were far fewer attorneys per capita, and advertising by attorneys was prohibited.

Early in 1966, Butchko attended the opening of the Arthur Carsten's headquarters in North Hollywood. Butchko indicated to people there his support for Carstens and passed out his own business cards.

Shortly before the primary, Butchko drove Arthur Carstens to a large rally for Governor Brown in Lancaster. Butchko spoke with many people. He supported Carstens, and passed out Carstens campaign cards. He also told people that he was running as a local candidate for the Los Angeles County Democratic Central Committee, and he passed out his own business cards.

The main power base of the pro-party establishment element had come to be the leadership of the labor organizations in the district. The leadership of the Machinists Union whose members worked at the large Lockheed aerospace plant in Burbank and elsewhere in the district was predominantly conservative on the issue of the war. Most of these Union leaders and other AFL-CIO leaders in the area were Masons. Butchko noted that the Masons were a strong group in the district. They were numerically very strong in the Antelope Valley areas and in Newhall, Saugus and the canyon areas nearby. They were numerically strong in Burbank and they tended to be strong and influential out of proportion to their numbers in the San Fernando Valley and Sunland and Tujunga portions of the district.

While the Masons did not openly practice politics as an organization, they were the most influential and powerful persons in the area of the Twenty-Seventh Congressional District and
throughout Southern California.

Most of the newspapers in the district were operated by Masons. The Valley Green Sheet, delivered four days a week to every residence in the San Fernando Valley was operated by Masons. The powerful Los Angeles Times was largely operated by Masons. Most of the newspapers in the district were Republican and conservative.

In 1966, most of the Masonically controlled newspapers throughout Southern California which took a position on the war in Vietnam either supported Johnson's general war policies or else favored more escalation.

In 1966 and 1967, Catholics were not permitted by their church to be Masons. This Church rule went back many years.

During the primary campaign, Reinecke, the beneficiary of Republican Party discipline, had no opposition. He took advantage of this situation by mounting a write-in campaign for himself in the Democratic Primary. He mailed special literature to

Democrats enclosing a ballpoint pen with the words "Write-in Reinecke" inscribed.

When the votes were counted, Reinecke received over 6,000 votes in the Democratic primary, a surprisingly high write-in vote. Howard received 17,911 votes. Carstens received 16,403 votes. Carstens ran ahead of Howard in the Forty-Second Assembly District where California Democratic Council precinct workers had walked a notable number of precincts on his behalf. Other candidates for the Democratic nomination received 6,940 votes, 4,023 votes and 2,712 votes respectively.

At the large pre-primary election party for Arthur Carstens in Van Nuys within a week or two before the June primary; Butchko was formally introduced as a California Democratic Council candidate for the Los Angeles County Democratic Central Committee.

Although Howard had won the Democratic Primary, most observers, including Butchko, decided on the basis of the primary votes that Reinecke would almost certainly win the general election. Butchko thought that Howard had won because a young Burbank attorney was preferred by the voters and because Howard had billboards. Butchko thought that many voters were confused as to the true facts about the war as well as to what the candidates stood for. Butchko thought that Johnson was seeking a military victory and he fully expected that the war would still be going on at the time of the 1968 elections.

In the June primary, Butchko was elected to the Los Angeles County Democratic Assembly District along with six other Democrats in the Sixty-Second Assembly District. He received 12,669 votes, first in the field. He was the only attorney in the field. The results of the race for County Democratic Central Committee in the

Sixty-Second Assembly District were published in the Burbank Daily Review showing Butchko first in the field with his vote total.

In the June primary, Assemblyman Morretti won renomination in the Forty-Second Assembly District by defeating a California Democratic Council endorsed and supported liberal named Gary Lipton. The California Democratic Council club members in the Forty-Second Assembly District did not like Morretti. As an Assemblyman, Morretti could avoid taking a public position on the war in Vietnam. As the peace movement continued its efforts in 1966 and 1967, Morretti did nothing to identify himself with it.

Right after the June 1966 primary, Butchko told Jeanne Caya that Butchko was planning to run against Reinecke in 1968, if Jack Howard did not win in 1966. Jeanne Caya eventually said that she approved of Butchko's plan.

In 1966 and 1967, Butchko had telephone conversations with Jeanne Caya on most days. They discussed politics, the peace movement, and Butchko's political plans. Butchko discussed with Jeanne Caya everything he did in politics. Jeanne Caya operated a beauty shop in Burbank and she talked about Butchko with her patrons.

After the June primary Butchko attended all of the meetings of the Burbank Democratic Club, and all of the meetings of the Twenty-Seventh Congressional District Democratic Council in 1966.

Butchko attended all of the meetings of the Los Angeles County Democratic Central Committee during his term, which extended to the June of 1968 primary election. At the first meeting of the Los Angeles County Democratic Central Committee attended by him, Butchko voted for Tom Bradley for Chairman of the Committee. Tom Bradley was supported by the California Democratic Council. His opponent, who won, was Billy Mills, who was supported by Jess Unruh. At this first meeting, Gordon Brucker, a member of the County Committee, from Lancaster, told Butchko that he thought his high vote was because Butchko was an attorney and the word; "attorney" was magic in the Antelope Valley. Jeannette MacFarland, another member of the County Committee from Butchko's District, told him that his high vote was due to his name.

In 1966, all of the members of Johnson's Cabinet were Anglo-Saxons.

Immediately after the primary, Howard sought the active support of the California Democratic Council Clubs whose candidate he had defeated. He would not alter his position on Vietnam. As a result, the clubs did not rush to endorse, and when they finally did, they gave him very little assistance. Club members did not work against him as some had done against Tom Bane two years earlier. Howard was deserted by many of his supporters from the primary. This made it obvious that they had merely wanted to use the Howard campaign to defeat Carstens. Nevertheless, Howard campaigned actively using billboards and mailers.

Shortly after the June 1966 primary election, Butchko attended the opening of Lorry Sherman's headquarters on Ventura Boulevard in Sherman Oaks. Lorry Sherman was a peace candidate. Butchko exchanged greetings with those present including Kazuo Unemoto and John Haggerty, the Democratic nominee for State Senator running against the Republican, Lou Cusanovich. John Haggerty said to Butchko that Jess Unruh was indirectly supporting and aiding Lou Cusanovich, the Republican incumbent.

Early in 1966, Butchko joined the Knights of Columbus, St. Cabrini Council in Burbank. In 1966 and 1967, Butchko was an active member of the Council. From the

15

latter part of 1966 into 1967, Butchko served as a member of the Board of Directors of the Cabrini Club, which board managed the building owned by the council.

On about Wednesday, July 20, 1966, Butchko attended a meeting of the Twenty-Seventh Congressional District Democratic Council. Carstens and Howard were both present. Butchko spoke very well to the entire group describing the method of arranging Brown-Anderson Neighborhood Centers as a campaign technique to aid their campaigns. Butchko was active in work to establish the Brown-Anderson Centers in the Sixty-Second Assembly District. An encaptioned picture was published in the Burbank Daily Review showing Burbank attorney John T. Butchko pointing out the location of the Brown-Anderson Neighborhood Centers to Lieutenant Governor Glen Anderson at a meeting of a Democratic group in the San Fernando Valley.

In the summer of 1966, Butchko attended the opening of the Sunland-Tujunga Democratic Clubs Headquarters on Foothill Boulevard, where he exchanged greetings with many of the persons in attendance, including the actor, John Forsythe. Butchko gave Mr. Forsythe his business card.

During the general election campaign of 1966, at a meeting of the Sunland-Tujunga Democratic Club, Butchko brought materials and spoke well on the procedures for setting up Brown-Anderson Neighborhood Centers. Howard also spoke at this meeting and said that he supported Johnson's Vietnam policy.

Butchko noted that in Reinecke's newsletter of September of 1966, mailed at government expense, Reinecke advocated the mining of Haiphong Harbor in North Vietnam, and Butchko fully expected that when he would run in 1968, the major issue between himself and Reinecke would be the issue of what to do about the war in Vietnam.

In November, Reinecke received 93,890 votes to 49,785 votes for Howard. At that time, there were approximately 109,000 registered Democrats and approximately 73,000 registered Republicans. Reinecke's official statement of campaign expenditures showed that the Congressman had spent over $80,000.

After the general election, Howard said to Butchko that Lorry Sherman, the Democratic peace candidate in the Twenty-Eighth Congressional District had been defeated by a larger margin than any Democrat in the history of that district.

In 1966, Butchko attended all of the meetings and parties of the Burbank Democratic Club. He also attended all of the meetings of the Burbank Bar Association. At all of the meetings of the Burbank Bar Association, Butchko spoke with attorneys and visitors. He also attended numerous parties and meetings of other Democratic groups.

Butchko saw that there were enormous obstacles in his planned effort to take Reinecke's Congressional District in 1968. The foremost of these were the danger of a gerrymander of the district, and the problem of raising enough money to win the primary and compete with the enormous campaign fund Reinecke would surely have in addition to the incumbent's free mailers.

Butchko also thought that Arthur Carstens would want to run again. Carstens continued to attend meetings and parties of California Democratic Council clubs in the district. Although Butchko had enthusiastically supported Carstens, he was determined to run in 1968, and he wished to dissuade Carstens from opposing him. Soon after the 1966 elections, rumors became widespread that Reinecke had made a deal with James

Corman, the incumbent Democratic Congressman from the adjoining Twenty-Second District encompassing San Fernando, Pacoima, and the western portion of the San Fernando Valley. The rumored deal was to transfer the most heavily Democratic portion of Reinecke's District to Corman's district, and to add to Reinecke's district some other area with a higher percentage of registered Republicans. The rumored deal was to become part of a reapportionment of all Congressional districts ordered by the California Supreme Court in order to comply with a ruling of the United States Supreme Court that Congressional Districts within a state must be of equal population.

In December of 1966, Butchko attended a California Democratic Council dinner at Robaires French Restaurant on Ventura Boulevard in Sherman Oaks, and was formally introduced as a member of the Los Angeles County Democratic Central Committee.

In December of 1966, Butchko attended a party sponsored by a California Democratic Council unit at a home in Saugus. Butchko told people there that he was planning to run for Congress in the Twenty-Seventh District in 1968. In 1967, Butchko was under much surveillance.

In January of 1967, at a heavily attended fundraising party sponsored by the Twenty-Seventh Congressional District Democratic Council at the United Auto Workers Hall in Van Nuys, Butchko was formally introduced as an elected member of the Los Angeles County Democratic Central Committee. Jeanne Caya then said, "Yea Butchko!" Candidates for the Los Angeles Board of Education were also introduced at that party. Travers Devine, who was supporting Butchko for Congress, did most of the work in arranging this party.

In 1967, Butchko attended all of the meetings of the Burbank Bar Association. In 1967, Butchko attended all of the meetings of the Twenty-Seventh Congressional District Democratic Council and all of the meetings of the Forty-Second Assembly District Democratic Council.

Butchko wrote letters to several Democratic members of the California State Legislature urging that the Twenty-Seventh Congressional District be left as a heavily Democratic District in registration so that a new Democrat could win in it. In those years, it was thought that a Congressional District required a 55% Democratic registration for a Democrat to win. State Senator Tom Carrell of San Fernando agreed that the district should be left as it was. Senator Carrell also told Butchko that he thought it would be fine for Butchko to seek the Twenty-Seventh Congressional District seat. Butchko felt that Tom Carrell was his best friend among the party establishment.

In 1967, before the California Democratic Committee Convention, Butchko met with Charles Waite, the anchorman for an important radio station. Waite said that as a member of the County Central Committee, Butchko had enough status to send out press releases. Butchko told Charles Waite that he was running against Reineke.

Early in 1967, Butchko told Jack Howard that Butchko would run for Congress against Reinecke in 1968.

In February of 1967, Butchko was elected vice-president of the Burbank Democratic Club, which had been held together for many years by Jeanne Caya. Travers

19

Devine was elected President of the Club. Travers was a few years younger than Butchko, but he had been active for years in the politics of the district. He had learned in the hard school of experience the problems, which Butchko would have to solve. Travers was familiar with the leaders of the California Democratic Council Clubs in the Twenty-Seventh District. Travers did press and publicity work for the statewide California Democratic Council organization, and he knew the reporters of the local newspapers. He would be valuable to Butchko's initial efforts, and he was willing to assist Butchko's bid for the Congressional Seat.

In about February of 1967, Butchko attended a strategy meeting of California Democratic members of the Los Angeles County Democratic Central Committee at Tom Bradley's home in Los Angeles.

In March of 1967, the statewide convention of the California Democratic Council was held in Fresno. The war in Vietnam was raging, and most of the delegates were determined to express their dissent from the war policies of the Johnson Administration. The Convention was also heavily attended by delegates who supported Johnson. At that time the California Democratic Council was a federation of grass roots clubs with 30,000 members all over the state of California.

Butchko drove himself, Travers and another delegate to the convention. An article was published in the Valley Green Sheet stating the names of delegates from the Burbank Democratic Club who would attend the convention, and stating that an eminent Burbank attorney, John Butchko would attend the convention as a delegate. The Valley Green Sheet was delivered to every residence in the San Fernando Valley and a part of Northwest Glendale.

20

At the California Democratic Council convention a resolution was passed favoring cessation of the bombing of North Vietnam and negotiations with the National Liberation Front. Butchko voted in favor of that resolution. At the convention, former Governor Pat Brown spoke and urged the delegates not to oppose the renomination of Lyndon Johnson.

At the final and dramatic day of the three day convention, the delegates passed, by a vote of 606 to 440 a resolution providing that the organization would hold a special convention in September of 1967, to establish machinery to select a slate of delegates to the Democratic National Convention pledged to support a candidate and a program opposed to the war policies of the Johnson Administration in Southeast Asia if there was no peaceful solution to the war by then. Butchko noted for the resolution, and he sensed that his vote had won for him the trust and confidence of the delegates from his district whose support was so important for him.

The delegates who voted for this resolution felt that they had advanced the peace movement to its highest point for the times, and they were delighted. The convention did seem to be a turning point. Public dissent from the war policies of the Johnson Administration increased at a more notable rate after the convention. By working in the Democratic Party of the largest State in the Union the peace movement had struck a sensitive nerve. The club members had a practical and effective goal toward which they would work. Many club members throughout the state who did not want to oppose the dominant leadership of the party establishment left the clubs of the California Democratic Council, and in some cases entire clubs noted to disaffiliate from the statewide organization. The State Chairman of the Democratic Party, Charles Warren, opposed the formation of a "peace slate", delegation by the California Democratic Council.

Throughout 1967, Butchko was the only declared candidate for the Democratic nomination for Congress in the Twenty-Seventh Congressional District.

Throughout 1967, Butchko was the front runner for the Democratic nomination for Congress in the Twenty-Seventh Congressional District.

In 1967, Butchko was more entrenched as a front-runner for the Democratic nomination for Congress in his district than any other person eyeing a Democratic nomination for Congress, excepting incumbent Congressman.

In 1967, Jeanne Caya told Butchko that she had been instrumental in getting Arthur Carstens to run for Congress in 1966. In 1967, Travers Devine told Butchko that Travers had been instrumental in getting Arthur Carstens to run for Congress in 1966.

Throughout 1967, Jeanne Caya told Butchko that she was supporting Butchko for the Democratic nomination for Congress in the Twenty-Seventh Congressional District. Throughout 1967, Travers Devine told Butchko that he was supporting Butchko for the Democratic nomination for Congress in the Twenty-Seventh Congressional District.

When Butchko returned to Burbank after the California Democratic Council convention in March of 1967, he had a discussion with Jack Howard. Jack Howard told Butchko that he had heard that Butchko had voted, at the California Democratic Council convention, for the resolution providing for a special convention in September to oppose the renomination of Lyndon Johnson if he had not ended the war by then. Jack Howard told Butchko that he (Jack Howard) resented that resolution.

22

Shortly after the March Convention, at the Smokehouse Restaurant in Burbank, Butchko had a meeting with Arthur Carstens and asked for his support. Arthur Carstens said to Butchko: "You have integrity. It shows through." Carstens said he would consider supporting Butchko provided that Butchko would run as a peace candidate. Butchko then felt confident that he would be able to get Carsten's support and the support of the California Democratic Council Clubs in the district.

Also shortly after the statewide California Democratic Council Convention, Butchko met with State Senator Tom Carrell, and Tom Carrell advised Butchko to get the endorsement of the California Democratic Council. Senator Carrell said that Butchko would have a hard time raising any money.

In 1967, there were published the results of various public opinion polls regarding the war in Vietnam. In all of these polls, a substantial number of persons favored a deeper escalation of the war effort. In all of these polls, a substantial number of people favored a continuation of the war policies of the Johnson Administration. In all of these polls, some persons favored views amounting to a de-escalation of the war. In all of these polls, the number of persons favoring a deeper escalation of the war effort combined with the number of persons focusing a continuation of Johnson's war policies were larger than the number of people favoring a de-escalation of the war. In at least one of these polls, the number of persons favoring a deeper escalation of the war was larger than the number of persons favoring de-escalation.

In about February of 1967, Butchko attended an open house party of the Burbank Human Relations Council on Burbank Boulevard in Burbank and talked with the members and visitors in attendance. Butchko then joined the Burbank Human Relations Council.

Throughout 1967, Butchko attended all of the meetings of the Forty-Second Assembly District Democratic Council and all of the meetings of the Twenty-Seventh Congressional District Democratic Council.

On the evening of the day of the outbreak of the 7 days Israel-Arab War, Butchko attended a meeting and party at the Valley Peace Center in Northridge. Butchko spoke with people there. Butchko told a leader of the Wayne Morse Democratic Club in the Forty-Second Assembly District that he was running for Congress against Reinecke. This gentleman told Butchko: "I am glad to hear it."

In January of 1967, Butchko told Richard Rogan, a former Chief Deputy Attorney General of California, and the owner of the building where Butchko's office was located, that Butchko was going to run for Congress against Reinecke. In January of 1967, Butchko told Jack Howard that Butchko was going to run for Congress against Reinecke.

In 1967, Culver Van Buren indicated to Butchko that he would support Butchko for Congress. Jeanne Caya had told Butchko that if he got Culver Van Buren, he would get Burbank. Culver Van Buren had been a President of the Burbank Bar Association, and he had the largest law practice of any attorney in Burbank.

In early 1967, Richard Rogan, Butchko's office landlord, told Butchko that he could use, free of charge, a vacant office suite on the third floor of the Rogan building as a campaign headquarters.

In the summer of 1967 Butchko told Eugene Radding that Butchko was going to run for Congress against Reinecke. Eugene Radding was Richard Rogan's law partner, and had been a Democratic nominee for Congress in the 20th Congressional District.

In 1967, Butchko represented the Burbank Human Relations Council at several meetings of the Community Relations Council of Southern California along with Ruth Spiegel, who subsequently became a President of the Burbank Human Relations Council, and also at a meeting of that Council in 1968.

In the spring of 1967, at a heavily attended banquet sponsored by the Sunland-Tujunga Democratic Club at the Tujunga Hotel Inn. Jeanne Caya was a featured speaker and in the course of her talk, she introduced Butchko and described him as the highest vote getter for County Committee in the Sixty-Second Assembly District.

Throughout 1967, Butchko sought to raise a campaign fund for his planned race for the Congressional seat. He was completely unable to raise any money. Few people thought that Reinecke could be defeated especially in what they expected to be a Republican year. In about the middle of 1967, Eugene Radding, a former candidate for Congress said to Butchko, "The Democratic Party is through. Nixon will win." But Butchko had confidence in his image.

In the summer of 1967, Butchko attended a California Democratic Council barbecue in the San Fernando Valley. He arrived after Jim Corman had attended the barbecue and left. Ted Lane told Butchko that Corman defended Johnson's Vietnam War policies. In 1966, Corman had been re-elected to Congress in the Twenty-Second Congressional District while supporting Johnson's Vietnam War policies. Butchko and Jo Seidita, the Secretary of the California Democratic Council, had a brief conversation and agreed that it would be useful to have a California Democratic Council peace candidate oppose Jim Corman in the 1968 Democratic primary.

In the late summer of 1967, Butchko attended a party for Democrats in the central valley. Howard Berman, the president of the California Federation of Young Democrats was there. Butchko told Mr. Berman that Butchko was going to run as a peace candidate against Ed Reinecke.

In the July or August issue of the "Progressive" magazine published by the Independent Young Democrats of the San Fernando Valley, a California Democratic Council Club, there was published an article by Butchko in which he described the planned peace slate delegation of the California Democratic Council and the positive effect it had on the peace movement, and praised those delegates to the March California Democratic Council convention who had voted to establish the planned peace slate delegation.

In August of 1967, Butchko made his first speech on Vietnam to a meeting of the Independent Young Democrats of the San Fernando Valley, a liberal California Democratic Council Club, at the Valley Peace Center in Northridge. Press releases preceding the speech were published in the Valley Green Sheet, the Burbank Daily Review and the Valley Times. These three newspapers all published Butchko's picture along with articles describing his background and stating that he would speak at the Independent Young Democratic Club of the San Fernando Valley at a certain address in Northridge, and that it was expected that he would deliver a major foreign policy address on Southeast Asian policy, and that it was expected that he would call for a major de-escalation of the war in Vietnam as a first step toward negotiations to end the war. In describing Butchko's background, these articles all stated that Butchko was an attorney in Burbank and an elected member of the Los Angeles County Democratic Central Committee, and that he was a graduate of the University of Southern California School of Law, where he was an associate editor of the Southern California Law Review; that he was a member of Phi Beta Kappa, and that he had served as a research attorney for the United States District Court for the Southern District of California.

The Valley Green Sheet was delivered to every residence in the San Fernando Valley and a large part of northwest Glendale.

Butchko's important publicity in 1967 discouraged Johnson from increasing the number of troops in Vietnam after July of 1967.

In his speech in August of 1967, Butchko delivered his full speech on Vietnam and attacked Reinecke as a hawk. In Butchko's full speech on Vietnam, he outlined in good detail the history of the war in Vietnam, and said in part that Vietnam was a united country for hundreds of years before the French conquered it; and that the Geneva Agreement of 1954 ending French involvement in Indochina provided that the French would withdraw from Vietnam and that the Southern portion of Vietnam was to be a temporary zone for the disembarcation of French troops, and that elections would be held in 1956 to unite Vietnam, and that the Saigon Government was established of violation of this treaty which had been signed by the United States as an observer, and that President Eisenhower opposed elections in Vietnam in 1956 because he thought Ho Chi Minh would win the elections; and that the war in Vietnam before and in 1965 was a struggle between large groups of South Vietnamese people aligned under the rival banners of the National Liberation Front and the Saigon Government, and that as it became clear that the Saigon Government was losing, United States participation increased, and the bombing of North Vietnam beginning in early 1965 preceded the large scale involvement of North Vietnamese fighting troops in the war in the South; and that entire villages suspected of harboring Viet Cong had come under attack in South Vietnam; and that the North Vietnamese would regard negotiations under bombing as a gesture of surrender that the leaders of that country were not willing to make; and that the United States involvement in the war was a tragic mistake; and that the demonstrations were not prolonging the war, but rather the bombing of North Vietnam was prolonging the war; and that war was being prolonged because of the excessive self regard of some of our national leaders who were unwilling to admit that they had made a mistake; and that Reinecke had called for escalation of the war in Vietnam and the mining of Haiphong harbor; and that we will seek to end the bombing of North Vietnam as a moral issue; and that we will continue our all out efforts to oppose the renomination of Lyndon Johnson; and we will act to elect peace candidates to Congress in every District where can possibly do so. Butchko also said that he was planning to run for Congress in the Twenty-Seventh Congressional District in 1968. Someone asked, "What if Arthur Carstens wants to run." Butchko replied that he would cross that bridge when he comes to it. By Butchko's major publicity for the speech he had taken a significant step toward establishing his public image and toward advancing the peace movement.

In 1967 and sometimes in 1968, Butchko practiced his speeches before he gave them.

As vice-chairman of the Burbank Democratic Club, Butchko presided over a meeting of the club at Roosevelt Junior High School in Burbank on August 16, 1967.

Butchko introduced David Scott, Sr., a recent candidate for Assembly and an effective speaker. Butchko also introduced Ben Leeds as a "leader of the peace movement in the Democratic Party". Ben Leeds was then the chairman of the Twenty-Seventh Congressional District Democratic Council.

In about August of 1967, Butchko attended a party at Helen Greenberg's home in Van Nuys. There he spoke with Congressman Tom Rees. Tom Rees said to Butchko that, "Congress is hawkish", but that he, Tom Rees, was dovish.

In the latter part of 1967, Jeanne Caya, who was supporting Butchko for Congress, told Butchko that she controlled Arthur Carstens, and that Arthur Carstens controlled Lorry Sherman.

On Saturday, August 26, 1967, at the California Democratic Council issues conference at San Fernando Valley State College in Northridge, Butchko took a leadership position. This issues conference was held preliminarily to the September Convention to select a peace slate delegation to oppose the renomination of Lyndon Johnson in the California Primary. One of the purposes of the issues conference was to develop proposals to be adopted at the September California Democratic Council special convention in Long Beach. At the foreign policy workshop of this issues conference, Butchko proposed a four-point program for ending United States military involvement in all of Vietnam. This included: 1. Immediate cessation of all bombing in all of Vietnam; 2. Immediate cessation of all offensive military operations by United States forces; 3. Offering to negotiate immediately with all parties including the NLF, and 4. Pledging complete withdrawal of all United States military forces as a result of these negotiations.

This proposal was passed by the vote of those present at the workshop. Arthur Carstens also attended this workshop. He stated at the workshop that he liked Butchko's program.

In September, the California Democratic Council held its special convention at the Long Beach Convention Center and proceeded to form a "peace slate" delegation to oppose Lyndon Johnson in the forthcoming 1968 primary. Butchko attended the convention as a delegate and voted for members of the "peace slate" delegation.

In 1967, Butchko's name was a political advantage for him.

Butchko attended a number of meetings of the Burbank Human Relations Council in 1967.

In the latter part of 1967, at a meeting of the Los Angeles County Democratic Central Committee attended by Butchko, Gilbert Lindsay, a Los Angeles City Councilman, introduced a resolution supporting President Lyndon Johnson. In a standing vote, Butchko voted against the resolution. The resolution was passed at the meeting.

Beginning in 1967, Charles Warren, the State Chairman of the Democratic Party was active in organizing the Lynch-Johnson Delegation for the 1968 Primary Election ballot; the members of the Lynch-Johnson Delegation took an oath to vote for Lyndon Johnson at the Democratic National Convention. Thomas Lynch was the Attorney General of California. The Lynch-Johnson delegation included many members of the Democratic Party establishment.

In November of 1967, Butchko spoke at a meeting of the Wayne Morse Democratic Club in the Forty-Second Assembly District. He said that he was running against Reinecke and he called for the election of aggressive peace candidates to Congress. When Ben Leeds arrived at this meeting, he asked if Butchko had spoken there. This showed that Ben Leeds, the Chairman of the Twenty-Seventh Congressional District Democratic Council, then recognized Butchko as the California Democratic Council candidate for Congress in that District. Butchko answered Ben Leeds and told him that he had already spoken at that meeting.

On Thanksgiving Day in 1967, the Valley Green Sheet published Butchko's picture along with an article stating, "Burbank attorney John Butchko, an elected member of the Los Angeles County Democratic Central Committee, has called for the establishment of equitable Congressional districting for the San Fernando Valley. The Valley comprises three districts, the 22nd, 27th and 28th."

"The state Legislature is presently under court order to redraw the congressional lines. It is expected that the eventual outcome will be districts that will be less in keeping with the "one man-one vote" edict and more along the typical gerrymandered lines drawn to protect the incumbent Congressman," Butchko said. In calling for equitable districts, Butchko said he would favor geographical cohesion over protecting officeholders of either party.'

"Butchko has communicated with numerous state legislators on the subject of drawing district lines, including State Sen. Tom Carrell and James Mills and Assemblymen, David Negri, Jack Fenton and Allen Sieroty."

"Butchko recently was praised by Sen. Robert F. Kennedy (D-N.Y.) for efforts on behalf of the Democratic Party."

In November of 1967, Butchko read an article by Senator Robert F. Kennedy in a popular national magazine in which Kennedy called for immediate cessation of the bombing of North Vietnam, but in this article Kennedy referred to the North Vietnamese Communists as aggressors.

In November of 1967, just before McCarthy announced his candidacy for President, the Valley Green Sheet and the Burbank Daily Review published articles stating that Butchko, an attorney in Burbank and an elected member of the Los Angeles County Democratic Central Committee and active member of the California Democratic Council, would speak at a meeting of the Burbank Democratic Club, and that it was expected that Butchko would urge immediate cessation of the bombing of North Vietnam as a first step toward negotiations to end the war and would urge support for the Presidential delegation of the California Democratic Council. These articles also state that a graduate of USC's School of Law, Butchko was an active member of many Burbank civic organizations. The article in the Burbank Daily Review also said that Butchko had been an associate editor of the Southern California Law Review. This was major publicity and a big boost for the peace movement. At this meeting, Butchko gave his full speech on Vietnam and stated that he expected that the California Democratic Council would now support McCarthy, and Butchko urged support for McCarthy. After his speech, Jeanne Caya said, "John Butchko, I love you."

As soon as McCarthy announced his candidacy for the Democratic nomination for President in November of 1968, Butchko sent him a letter of support, and received a friendly reply letter from Senator McCarthy.

In about November of 1967, Butchko attended a fundraising party for John Burton, who was running in a special election for the State Senate as a peace candidate in San Francisco. Butchko told the people there, including Assemblyman, Allen Sieroty, that he was running for Congress against Reinecke. Jeanne Caya told Butchko that he "took over this party." Burton lost his election in San Francisco, but remained a State Assemblyman.

In December, Butchko attended a meeting of the Sunland-Tujunga Democratic Club and made a statement before the entire group favorable to the peace slate delegation of the California Democratic Council, which would become the McCarthy delegation in the California primary.

Later in December, Butchko attended a meeting of the peace slate steering committee in North Hollywood and made a statement before the entire group favorable to the peace slate delegation of the California Democratic Council, which was then becoming the McCarthy delegation; Butchko also told a number of people at this meeting that he would run for Congress in 1968.

In December of 1968, at the Pickwick Banquet Room in Burbank, David Schonbrun made a major foreign policy speech criticizing Johnson's Vietnam War policies and expressing his support for McCarthy and the California Democratic Council peace slate delegation. Butchko attended the banquet at which this speech was delivered. Travers Devine arranged the local publicity for this event in which Butchko, as vice-president of the Burbank Democratic Club, was described as a co-sponsor of the banquet. This publicity appeared in an article published in the Burbank Independent and Glendale Independent.

The 1967 session of the state legislature was adjourned without any redistricting of the Congressional seats. For a time, it looked as though the Twenty-Seventh District would remain heavily Democratic in registration. But the State Supreme Court then ruled

33

that if the Legislature did not exact a valid reapportionment measure by December 7, 1967, the Court would order into effect a reapportionment plan of its own.

The legislature met in a special session later in December and redrew the district lines. After considering several reapportionment measures, the legislature approved the so called "incumbents' plan" in December. It was publicly announced by proponents of the plan that it was designed to protect all the incumbent Congressmen, by giving them more of their own party's registration. Assemblyman Jack Fenton, a sponsor of the incumbents' plan stated with respect to reapportionment measures: "they will all be sweetheart bills to perpetuate those in office." At the time of the reapportionment, Democrats held a slight majority in the State Assembly, while the State Senate was evenly divided.

The California Supreme court proceeded to review the legislature's plan. Butchko filed a brief with the Court urging that the legislature's reapportionment plan was invalid. However, the Court upheld the validity of the legislature's plan. Time was running short for the County Clerks and Registrar of Voters offices to make the necessary preparations for the 1968 elections.

The legislatures plan protected Corman by placing the heavily Democratic Forty-Second Assembly District in the Twenty-Second Congressional District. The reapportionment placed into the Twenty-Seventh Congressional District most of the Sixty-Fourth Assembly District, including the West Valley Communities of Chatsworth, Canoga Park, Winnetka, Northridge and Granada Hills and Porter Ranch. The area had only a very small Democratic edge in registration, and it has been in Corman's district. The plan also transferred into the Twenty-Seventh Congressional District Sherman Oaks,

Studio City, Toluca Lake and some adjoining areas in the southern San Fernando Valley. These areas had formerly been represented by a Republican Congressman, Alfonzo Bell. In addition, the Twenty-Seventh Congressional District acquired portions of Kern County east of the Los Angeles Aqueduct, including Ridgecrest and China Lake, where a naval weapons base was located, California City, Mojave, Boron, Rosamond and Edwards Air Force Base.

The Twenty-Seventh District retained those portions of the Sixty-Second Assembly

District, which had previously been in the Twenty-Seventh, that is, a large portion of Burbank, all of Sunland and Tujunga and the northern portion of Los Angeles County.

An article in the Wall Street Journal declared that the new Twenty-Seventh Congressional District was the most gerrymandered district in the United States. It is no wonder; the new district included large portions of the west, south and east San Fernando Valley, in a horseshoe design almost surrounding Corman's now safe Twenty-Second Congressional District. The Twenty-Seventh District embraced some fifty-two communities. The West Valley portion of the District was connected to the northern portion in a mountainous area where there was no road connecting those portions of the district.

The new district had over 600,000 people and 4,000 square miles. The new district had a Democratic registration of about 51% of the two-party designation. In California, it had traditionally been felt that a Democrat needed a 55% Democratic registration in order to win. Although Reinecke now appeared to be in a much better position than before, he publicly complained about the redistricting on the ground that it

35

caused him to lose some of his former constituency. It was promptly reported in the Newhall Signal, a liberal newspaper in the District, that Reinecke was creating quite a credibility gap by this complaint. Butchko heard through the grapevine that Reinecke was pleased with the new district.

In December after the redistricting, Butchko attended a party at Helen Greenberg's home in Van Nuys. Assemblyman Morretti was there and spoke. He said that one good thing about the redistricting was that it protected Congressman Corman. Los Angeles City Councilman Ernarndi Bernardi also spoke at this party and said that former Governor Brown and Mayor Yorty were both supporting Johnson.

In December of 1967, Butchko attended the large Christmas Party at Dick Rogan's house in Burbank, where he told people that he was running for Congress against Reinecke. Richard Nevins, a member of the State Board of Equalization and a Democrat told Butchko that he was supporting Johnson.

In late December, Butchko attended a party sponsored by the Reseda-West Valley Democratic Club and told many people that he was running as a peace candidate for the Democratic nomination for Congress in the new Twenty-Seventh District. Assemblyman, David Negri, of San Fernando was also at this party. Nick Seidita, the husband of Jo Seidita, the Secretary of the California Democratic Council, said to Butchko that he could understand it if George Brown supported Johnson for renomination.

The new Twenty-Seventh District had a lower percentage of Black votes than any Congressional District in the country.

In December of 1967, Jack Howard said to Butchko that when Howard was running for Congress against Reinecke in 1966, the newspapers would not publish his press releases.

In 1968, Butchko was under much surveillance. This helped make Butchko be the most effective peace candidate.

On the day of Butchko's speech in January at the meeting of the Studio City Democratic Club, John Clancy called Butchko and said that he wanted Butchko to meet with a gentleman in Newhall who had some damaging information on Reinecke.

Butchko knew Clancy. In 1966 Clancy sought unsuccessfully the Democratic nomination for Assembly in the 62nd Assembly District. Butchko took Clancy up on his offer. Butchko, Travers and Clancy drove out to the Newhall Bowl in Newhall where Butchko and Travers were introduced by Clancy to Mr. N. Mr. N told Butchko that he was unofficially representing the L.A. County Federation of Labor, AFL-CIO, which was going to support the pro-Johnson delegation, headed by Attorney General Tom Lynch. Mr. N drove Butchko and Clancy to Mr. N's home in Newhall. Mr. N wore a Masonic pin. Mr. N said that he realized that Johnson could not carry California against Nixon but that he did not want to lose it by too much.

Mr. N said that the L.A. County Federation of Labor had been looking for a candidate to run against Butchko but that they could not find anyone. He asked Butchko if he would support Johnson for renomination. Butchko said that he was supporting McCarthy and would continue to support McCarthy.

Mr. N said that Johnson knew that he could not carry California against Nixon, but that he did not want to lose it by too much. Mr. N said that he hoped that Butchko would not fight the establishment too hard in his campaign. Mr. N said that he would not believe that Lyndon Johnson had anything to do with assassination of John F. Kennedy unless he was presented documentary evidence proving it in black and white. He said that he knew Butchko had some five hundred precinct workers and Mr. N hoped that their course of campaigning for Butchko they would not say that Johnson had something to do with the assassination of John F. Kennedy.

Butchko said that he would only ask his campaign workers to say those things that were calculated to help him win his election. Mr. N seemed satisfied with that answer.

Lionel Rolfe, a Newhall Signal reporter than arrived and joined the discussions. The Signal and Mr. Rolfe were favorably inclined to Butchko's candidacy because of his position on Vietnam. Mr. N then proceeded to outline the information, which would damage Reinecke. Mr. N said that a woman employee of an industrial plant had written Reinecke complaining about working conditions at her plant; that was fired shortly thereafter; and that she was told it was because of a letter she wrote. He gave the Lancaster address of this lady, and he said that the Newhall Signal had possession of her letters to the Newhall Signal explaining all of the details, and that Mr. N would advise the Signal to let Butchko have access to these. Mr. N said that this information would get Butchko through the primary.

Butchko said that he wanted to take some time to consider whether he could use the story. Mr. N said that since Butchko would not support Johnson, he would not get any money from the L.A. County Federation of Labor, AFL-CIO, but that he would see if he could at least get the L.A. County Federation of Labor to endorse Butchko.

Eugene McCarthy had stated that 1968 would be the year of confrontation over the war in Vietnam. During the last week in November of 1967, former President Eisenhower proposed a limited ground invasion of North Vietnam to knock out artillery shelling of United States forces just south of the demilitarized zone separating North and South Vietnam.

In December of 1967, Mary Bockwinkel said to Butchko that she was somewhat disappointed by McCarthy because he had said that favored cessation of bombing only in some parts of North Vietnam, on television.

The political confrontation had already begun to take shape in the Twenty-Seventh Congressional District. Charles Warren, an Assemblyman from Hollywood and State Chairman of the Democratic Party of California, had announced the formation of Democratic Campaign Committees for regional districts corresponding approximately to the states Congressional Districts, prior to the September special convention of the California Democratic Council. Butchko and other active Democrats received invitations to participate. Butchko was advised by several of his supporters in California Democratic Council clubs including Jeanne Caya that the official Democratic Campaign Committee being formed by Mr. Warren was a threat to his campaign. Warren was billing the plan as a unity effort in which all Democrats could participate since it would work for goals common to all Democrats, such as the success of Democratic campaigns in the general elections. At a meeting of the Democrats in the Twenty-Seventh District called by Warren and attended by Butchko, Warren said that whether the California Democratic

Council members would participate or not, he would go ahead with organizing the Committee for the district. After the meeting and on September 27, 1967, Warren sent a letter to all of the Democrats who had been invited to participate, in which he announced the appointment of a certain young attorney, Leonard Dubin, to the position of Co-Chairman of the Campaign for Region 26, which corresponded to the Twenty-Seventh Congressional District. Butchko knew this appointee and knew that he had exposed an interest in running for Congress in 1968. In fact he had told Butchko himself that he might run if the district was not gerrymandered. Butchko thought that this potential candidate would be able to use his position as Co-Chairman of the committee to advance his own standing in the district to the disadvantage of Butchko's standing. Dubin had voted against the resolution which led to the California Democratic Council's peace slate Presidential delegation at the March 1967 California Democratic Council convention. Butchko complained to Warren about the appointment of Dubin but to no avail. Butchko was sure that this preferment of a potential rival was attributable to the fact that Butchko was then openly supporting the California Democratic Council's presidential delegation while his rival had not yet been known to support it. When the Twenty-Seventh Congressional District was gerrymandered, Butchko heard no more of this so-called Democratic Campaign Committee for Region 26. Throughout 1967 Butchko was running for Congress as a peace candidate. Also in 1967 Butchko was a leader in the peace movement.

On Saturday, December 30, 1967, Butchko mailed his announcement of candidacy to numerous newspapers. Butchko's announcement of candidacy was published in the Los Angeles Times in at least the San Fernando Valley Section, the

Valley Green Sheet, the Valley Times, the Newhall Signal, the Northridger, the Newhall-Saugus Sun and Sylmar Breeze, the Daily Ledger Gazette, the Antelope Valley Press, the Burbank Daily Review, the Glendale Star News and on the front page of a special edition newspaper delivered to every residence in the San Fernando Valley, except for the far northern portion, on the first Saturday in January. These articles all stated that John T. Butchko had announced that he is a candidate for the Democratic nomination for Congress in the Twenty-Seventh Congressional District. These articles all stated that Butchko was an attorney in Burbank and an elected member of the Los Angeles County Democratic Central Committee and described Butchko's background and stated that he was a member of Phi Beta Kappa, and that he was a graduate of the University of Southern California School of Law where he was an associate editor of the Southern California Law Review, and that he had served as a research attorney for the United States District Court for the Southern District of California. These articles announcing Butchko's candidacy all stated that in speeches on foreign policy, Butchko had called for immediate cessation of the bombing of North Vietnam as a first step toward negotiations to end the war. Almost all of these articles also stated that Butchko was an active member of numerous civic organizations. Some of the articles, including the article in the Los Angeles Times also stated that Butchko was a member of the Order of the Coif, an honorary legal fraternity. Some of these articles also stated that Butchko was a graduate of Glendale High School. All of these articles announcing Butchko's candidacy were accompanied by his picture except for the article in the Burbank Daily Review and the Glendale Star News.

41

The Newhall-Saugus Sun and Sylmar Breeze was delivered in Newhall-Saugus, and Valencia and the surrounding Canyons, and Sylmar. On Wednesday, it was delivered to every residence in these areas.

The Glendale Star-News was delivered to every residence in Glendale.

The article announcing Butchko's candidacy in the Daily Ledger-Gazette was published on Wednesday. That newspaper was delivered to every residence in the Antelope Valley.

The Antelope Valley Press was delivered to every residence in the Antelope Valley. The Valley Green Sheet was delivered to every residence in the San Fernando Valley and part of Northwest Glendale.

The article announcing Butchko's candidacy in the Newhall Signal began on the front page where it was published a caption under Butchko's picture stating "John Butchko: Viet Dove." This article also contained statements from an interview with Butchko and stated that Butchko regarded Johnson and Reinecke as hawks. The article in the Newhall Signal also stated that if elected in November, Butchko would be 31 years of age and one of the youngest members of Congress.

The Newhall Signal was circulated in Newhall, Saugus, Valencia and the surrounding canyon areas. The special edition newspaper delivered to every residence in the San Fernando Valley except for the far northern portion, on the first Saturday in January placed the article announcing Butchko's candidacy along with his picture on its front page.

All this publicity for Butchko had a tremendous effect on advancing the peace movement.

In 1968 Butchko's name made people think of revolution. This made Butchko a tremendously effective peace candidate.

In January of 1968, as chairman of the bylaws committee of the Council, Butchko prepared the bylaws of the Twenty-Seventh Council District Democratic Council. These bylaws were approved and adopted by a special meeting of the Twenty-Seventh Council District Democratic Council in January.

Early in January, Butchko had a meeting with State Senator Anthony Bielenson. Bielenson told Butchko that getting elected to Congress required a greater effort than getting elected to the Los Angeles County Democratic Central Committee, but that with Butchko's name, he was not sure that this would be true in Butchko's case.

In 1968, a Russian-American image seemed better than any other kind of American image and that fact gave tremendous strength to Butchko's candidacy. In 1968, the regular Masons did not allow Blacks as members of the Masons.

Travers Devine worked as Butchko's campaign manager from the beginning of January 1968 through the June primary. Travers spent most of his days in Butchko's law office and on many nights beginning in January he put up Butchko's campaign signs in the district. Travers accompanied Butchko on most of his speaking engagements and appearances.

In January of 1968, Travers Devine told Butchko that Travers had organized and led anti-Vietnam war demonstrations at San Fernando Valley State College in Northridge.

On a Sunday in early January, Butchko appeared at a party at the Valley Peace Center in Northridge where he rounded up supporters.

43

In January, Butchko spoke on two successive nights to different shifts of the Burbank Firefighters at a Union Hall in Burbank. In the second of these speeches, Butchko attacked Johnson's Vietnam War policies, and criticized Reinecke as a hawk.

In January, Butchko appeared at a meeting of a California Democratic Council Unit at Bill Morosoff's home in Sherman Oaks. Bill Morosoff said to the entre group there: "John Butchko is here."

In January, Butchko appeared at a party for friends of Jo Seidita in the West Valley. Butchko there passed out his campaign cards. Butchko rounded up supporters, and told a lady there that he was also opposed to United States bombing in South Vietnam. Some women there pinned Butchko's campaign cards on their blouses.

Throughout 1968, Butchko received much publicity in the Valley Green Sheet and in the Newhall Signal, and in the Reminder newspaper. The Reminder was circulated in Woodland Hills.

In January of 1968, Jim Corman, the Democratic Congressman for the Twenty-Second District in the central San Fernando Valley stated on Radio Station KGIL, the Valley station, that he favored the bombing of North Vietnam.

In 1968, Chuck Manatt became Corman's campaign treasurer.

Early in January, Butchko attended a large banquet sponsored by the Burbank Bar Association at the Pickwick Banquet Hall and he told people there that he was running for Congress against Reinecke. Butchko also attended the regular meeting of the Burbank Bar Association in January.

In January of 1968, the Newhall Signal published an article stating that Butchko favored preservation of our redwood forests, our national parks and our wilderness areas.

44

In late January or early February, Culver Van Buren said to Butchko that he would help with Butchko's campaign.

In the 1950's and 1960's Catholics were taught to pray for the conversion of Russia. This added strength to Butchko's candidacy in 1967 and 1968.

In January of 1968, Liz Atkerson, the manager of the Burbank Legal Aid and Lawyers Reference Service, told Butchko that many people told her that they liked Butchko as a candidate because of his name.

In 1968, Jerry Brown, the son of the former Governor, was not running for any office.

In February Butchko spoke at a meeting of the Studio City Democratic Club at a hall in Studio city. An article in the Valley Green Sheet announced that Butchko would give this speech and stated that Butchko was an attorney in Burbank and an elected member of the Los Angeles County Democratic Central Committee, and also described some of Butchko's background. At this meeting, Butchko gave his full speech on Vietnam. This was a large California Democratic Council Club. After the speeches Butchko told a recent candidate for city council in Burbank that we are turning Burbank into a peace slate city. This man was also an attorney.

Lorry Sherman, the Treasurer of the California Democratic Council joined in the applause for Butchko's speech. Lorry Sherman said that McCarthy was not yet that good candidate that we wanted him to be but, that we (The California Democratic Council) would make him be that good candidate.

In January of 1968 on the first day of filing for office Butchko attended a Petition Party for Eugene McCarthy at a home in Burbank. Butchko passed out his campaign cards to everyone there and told them that he was running for Congress against Reinecke. Butchko signed an official petition to place McCarthy on the ballot in California.

In January, Butchko attended a planning meeting of the peace state Steering Committee for the San Fernando Valley at the United Auto Workers Hall in Van Nuys, and passed out his campaign cards, and spoke with some people. The Record Ledger and the Glendale Independent published an article stating that Butchko would speak at a meeting of the Reseda-West Valley Democratic Club on January 17 at a home in Canoga Park. The article in the Glendale Independent published Butchko's picture along with this article. The Glendale Independent was delivered to most residences in Glendale. At this meeting, Butchko gave his full speech on Vietnam. After Butchko's speech, a man with a Hispanic surname said that he liked the candidate.

In About February of 1968, Butchko spoke at a meeting of the San Fernando Valley State College Democratic Club at San Fernando Valley State College in Northridge. At this meeting, Butchko gave his full speech on Vietnam. After his speech, Butchko was interviewed by a reporter, and his comments on Vietnam were published in an article in the San Fernando Valley State College Sundial.

In February 1968, the TET Offensive ended in a crushing defeat for the Communists. In February, Butchko was interviewed by the interviewing committee of the Los Angeles County Federation of Labor interviewing committee for the San Fernando Valley. Butchko did well, and this interviewing committee recommended that the L.A. County Federation of Labor endorse Butchko.

In February or March, Butchko appeared at a meeting sponsored by the Northridge Democratic Club, and he then passed out his campaign cards.

46

In February, Butchko spoke at a meeting of a large Young Democratic Club, not affiliated with the California Democratic Council, at the Kester Avenue Elementary School in Van Nuys. Butchko gave his full speech on Vietnam at this meeting. An article in the Valley Green Sheet announced that Butchko would give this speech and described Butchko's background. In this speech, Butchko also said that the bombing of North Vietnam was immoral.

In January or February, Butchko appeared at a party sponsored by the Burbank Democratic Club. An article in the Valley Green Sheet announced that Butchko would appear at this party and described some of Butchko's background.

In January or February, Butchko attended a meeting of the Sunland-Tujunga Democratic Club, and spoke with people there.

In January, Butchko spoke at a meeting of the Northwest Valley Democratic Club. Butchko gave his full speech on Vietnam at this meeting. An article in the Valley Green Sheet announced that Butchko would speak at this meeting and described some of Butchko's background.

In February, Lyndon Johnson received 49% or 47% of the popular vote in the New Hampshire Presidential primary, and Eugene McCarthy received 42% of the popular vote. This was a surprisingly high vote for McCarthy.

Immediately after the New Hampshire primary, Culver Van Buren came into Butchko's office and said: "You were right about the war in Vietnam. There is a lot of resentment against it."

In February, Butchko spoke at a meeting of the Soledad Township Democratic Club at a home in Saugus. Butchko gave his full speech on Vietnam at this meeting. An

47

article in the Newhall Signal announced that Butchko would give this speech and called Butchko a "peace candidate," and stated that Butchko was supporting Eugene McCarthy.

In 1967 and in 1968 Butchko's speeches on the war in Vietnam had the effect of moving the country.

In early April the Glendale Independent published an article stating that John T. Butchko had filed as a candidate for the Democratic nomination for Congress in the Twenty-Seventh Congressional District, and that Butchko, a Burbank attorney, charged that Reinecke actively promoted the redrawing of district lines to protect himself from the voters who had come to know his poor record, and that Butchko stated that Reinecke had imprudently advocated escalation and the mining of Haiphong Harbor and that in speeches on foreign policy given to numerous civic organizations, Butchko had consistently called for immediate cessation of the bombing of North Vietnam as a first step toward negotiations to end the war, and that Butchko said, "A peacetime economy will provide new opportunities for tax reduction and increased business growth." The article also described Butchko's educational and professional background. This article also stated that Butchko was a member of the Burbank Democratic Club, the Burbank Bar Association, the Burbank Human Relations Council and the Burbank Chamber of Commerce.

The Glendale News Press also published an article stating in part that Butchko had filed to run for Congress in the Twenty-Seventh Congressional District, as a Democrat, and described Butchko as an attorney in Burbank.

In March or April, Butchko appeared at a meeting of a California Democratic Council Club located mostly in the central valley, but some of whose members lived in the Twenty-Seventh Congressional District. Butchko was introduced as the Democratic candidate for Congress in the Twenty-Seventh Congressional District.

In January, Butchko appeared at the offices of the San Fernando Valley Fair Housing Council on Ventura Boulevard in Sherman Oaks. He then joined that Council as a member. He spoke with the people there and left them a stack of his campaign cards. In the next newsletter of that Council, it was stated that "our new member, John Butchko is running for Congress in the Twenty-Seventh Congressional District. Good luck, John."

In all of his speeches given to California Democratic Council clubs in 1967 and in 1968 and in his speech at the endorsing convention of the Twenty-Seventh Congressional District Democratic Council in March, Butchko stated "We will continue our all out effort to oppose the renomination of Lyndon Johnson, and to elect Democratic peace candidates to Congress in every district where we can possibly do so."

In the many articles in the Valley Green Sheet during the primary campaign it was stated that Butchko was an attorney in Burbank and an elected member of the Los Angeles County Democratic Central Committee. Before the close of filing these articles stated that he was a candidate for the Democratic nomination for Congress in the Twenty-Seventh Congressional District. After the close of filing these articles stated that he was the Democratic candidate for Congress in the Twenty-Seventh Congressional District.

In February, the Newhall Signal published an article stating that Butchko charged that Reinecke had imprudently advocated escalation of the war in Vietnam and the mining of Haiphong Harbor and that Reinecke did not have the ability to deal with difficult problems of foreign affairs, and that Butchko had consistently called for

49

immediate cessation of the bombing of North Vietnam as a first step toward negotiations to end the war.

In March of 1968, Butchko attended the wedding of Bob and Mary Bockwinkel in the West Valley. Bob and Mary Bockwinkel were the leaders of the Independent Young Democrats of the San Fernando Valley, a California Democratic Council club. After the wedding, Butchko attended the reception at a church hall in the West Valley, where he did some political campaigning and passed out his campaign cards.

Starting in January and throughout the 1968 campaign, Butchko did a good job of keeping up his campaign signs, including one sheets, quarter cards, and some bumper stickers throughout the San Fernando Valley portion of his district and in Sunland and Tujunga. He also had some signs put up in the Antelope Valley. To Snipe means to put up political signs.

In March, Mary Lou Howard, Jack Howard's wife, came into Butchko's office and said she saw Butchko signs everywhere.

In March on the evening before the endorsing convention of the Twenty-Seventh Congressional District Democratic Council, Butchko appeared at a party of the Independent Young Democrats of the San Fernando Valley at a home in the West Valley.

On March 10, at San Fernando Valley State College, at the endorsing convention of the Twenty-Seventh Congressional District Democratic Council, Jeanne Caya spoke in favor of Butchko and stated that he had always been for peace. Dorothy Bereny, the California Democratic Council endorsed candidate for Assembly in the Fifty-Seventh Assembly District, then spoke in favor of Butchko and stated that he had always helped the California Democratic Council. Butchko then gave his full speech on Vietnam

50

and made other statements about the role of the California Democratic Council in the peace movement. There was then a question and answer period. Someone asked Butchko," What will you do after you end the war in Vietnam?" Butchko answered: "I will improve our relations with the Soviet Union." Butchko was asked what he would do with our air bases in Thailand. Butchko said he would remove them. The convention voted 41 to 27 to endorse Butchko. There was some opposition to Butchko by some primadonnas, including Jo Seidita. Sixty percent of the votes were required for endorsement. Butchko got over sixty percent of the vote.

David Scott, Sr., a Black man, and a former candidate for Assembly, presided at this endorsing convention. After Butchko was endorsed, Mr. Scott said to the endorsing convention: "What you did here today will have reverberations in the White House."

Travers told Butchko that his speech had got him the endorsement. Travers told Butchko that the Young Democrats were fired up by his speech.

After Butchko was endorsed by the Twenty-Seventh Congressional District Democratic Council in March, Butchko wrote to Senator McCarthy informing McCarthy that Butchko had been endorsed by the Council and that it then appeared that Butchko would be unopposed for the Democratic nomination for Congress. Butchko soon received a reply letter from McCarthy, in which McCarthy stated that he was pleased to know of the progress of Butchko's campaign.

The Valley Green Sheet published five of Butchko's press releases in 1968 before the first bombing halt on March 31, 1968.

In 1968, Butchko made many visits to headquarters, and appeared at many headquarters meetings.

The Newhall Signal published six articles on Butchko before the first bombing halt on March 31, 1968.

In 1967 Butchko was under much surveillance.

In 1967 and in 1968, Butchko's speeches on the war in Vietnam had the effect of moving the country.

The year of 1968 was the turning point in the debate about the war in Vietnam.

When the Twenty-Seventh Congressional District Democratic Council endorsed Butchko in the middle of March, articles stating that fact along with Butchko's statement calling for immediate cessation of the bombing of North Vietnam were published in the Hollywood Citizen-News, the Beverly Hills Edition of the Hollywood Citizen News, the Valley Times, the Record Ledger and the Montrose Ledger and the Reminder and the Northridger. The articles in the Hollywood Citizen News, the Beverly Hills Edition of the Hollywood Citizen-News, the Valley Times and the Record Ledger and the Reminder and the Northridger also included a statement of Butchko's background and his attack on Reinecke as a hawk. The articles in the Hollywood-Citizen News, the Beverly Hills Edition of the Hollywood Citizen News, the Valley Times and the Record Ledger and the Reminder and the Northridger stated in part: "Butchko is an attorney in Burbank and an elected member of the Los Angeles County Democratic Central Committee.

"Butchko told the convention that he would wage an aggressive campaign on the major issues to unseat the incumbent, Edwin Reinecke."

"Butchko called for immediate cessation of the bombing of North Vietnam as a first step toward negotiations to end the war. Butchko stated that Reinecke has imprudently called advocated escalation and the mining of Haiphong Harbor.' Butchko said: 'It is time to elect a new Congressman with a better understanding of foreign relations.'

"Butchko is an active member of numerous civic organizations, including membership in the Burbank Bar Association, the Burbank Chamber of Commerce, the Burbank Human Relations Council and the Burbank Democratic Club.'

"Butchko graduated from the University of Southern California Law School, where he was an associate editor of the Southern California Law Review. He is also a member of Phi Beta Kappa and the Order of the Coif, an honorary legal fraternity. Butchko has served as a research attorney for the United States District Court for the Southern District of California. His practice and home are both in Burbank.'

"Butchko has promised to take the 'issues to the people and to expose the incumbent's lack of ability to deal with difficult national problems.' Butchko said that the incumbent must share the responsibility for inflation and higher taxes."

The Montrose Ledger, also called the Ledger, was delivered in the Crescenta Valley, including Sunland and Tujunga.

The Record Ledger was delivered in Sunland and Tujunga.

The Hollywood Citizen-News was delivered in the Hollywood area. These articles were published in early April. But Butchko mailed these press releases on March 10 right after his endorsement.

Shortly after Butchko's endorsement for the Twenty-Seventh Congressional District Democratic Council and on March 16, 1968, Senator Robert Kennedy, after a conversation with Jess Unruh, stated that he would be a candidate for President in 1968. At all prior times, Kennedy had stated that he would not be a candidate for President in

1968. Robert Kennedy had never endorsed McCarthy. Jesse Unruh became Robert Kennedy's campaign manager for California.

In March, shortly after Senator Robert F. Kennedy announced his candidacy for President, Newhall Signal published an interview with Butchko which stated that Butchko said that he had supported McCarthy early and would continue to support him, but that he regarded Kennedy as a peace candidate and that he would support Kennedy if he won the Democratic nomination for President.

March 22, 1968, was the last day of filing for the primary. Being unopposed in the Democratic primary made Butchko a tremendously effective peace candidate.

No one had filed to run for Congress in the Twenty-Seventh Congressional District as a candidate of the newly formed Peace and Freedom Party. This was very unusual in California.

William Gayle, of Saugus, and Jim Miller of Lancaster had filed as candidates for the Republican nomination for Congress in the Twenty-Seventh district opposing Reinecke for the Republican nomination.

Mildred Simon filed as a Democrat to run against Jim Corman in the Twenty-Second Congressional District. Mildred Simon was a peace candidate, endorsed by the Twenty-Second Congressional District Democratic Council.

Butchko thought that he was unopposed in the primary because of his name and his political ability.

On March 22, the date of the close of filing, Butchko appeared at a party at the home of a young Democrat in the West Valley. It was like a victory celebration for Butchko. Mildred Simon was there. Butchko spoke with people at this party.

In late March of 1968, the California Democratic Council held its state convention at the Anaheim Convention Center. The convention voted to support McCarthy, and to endorse Anthony Bielensen for United States Senate. Joe Wulf, an officer of the California Democratic Council, introduced Butchko to the convention as the California Democratic Council endorsed candidate for Congress in the Twenty-Seventh Congressional District and stated that, "We hope he wins" (referring to Butchko). On an evening during the convention, Butchko spoke at a caucus of delegates from the Twenty-Seventh Congressional District, and, among other things, stated that he would conduct an aggressive campaign and that he would win in November.

At the time of the convention, McCarthy stated his contest with Bobby was a struggle for control of the Democratic Party in California between his friends in the California Democratic Council and Jesse Unruh.

Before appearing at a meeting in Val Verde on the same day, a Sunday, Butchko attended a meeting of the executive board of the Soledad Township Democratic Club, where he told Jeannette MacFarland that he was officially unopposed in the primary.

In late March of 1968, Butchko appeared at a meeting of Democrats in Val Verde. An article in the Newhall Signal announced that Butchko would appear there. Butchko spoke with people at this meeting.

On March 31, Lyndon Johnson stated in a nationally televised address that he was withdrawing from the Presidential contest, and that he was stopping the bombing of most of North Vietnam (all of North Vietnam except for the small southern portion).

55

The movement to prevent the renomination of Lyndon Johnson would not have succeeded without the effects of Butchko's campaign. There would nave been no bombing halt without the effect of Butchko's campaign.

Butchko's aggressive campaign for Congress was the major factor in the movement, which induced Johnson to stop the bombing of most of North Vietnam on March 31, 1968. After this partial bombing halt Johnson and North Vietnam had preliminary peace talks, but full negotiations were not started until the final bombing halt on October 31, 1968.

After Johnson stopped bombing most of North Vietnam on March 31, the Newhall Signal published an article stating that in an interview Butchko had been quoted as stating that the bombing halt of most of North Vietnam was a step in the right direction and that the leaders of North Vietnam would not negotiate under bombing because they would regard that as a gesture of surrender.

At the time of the bombing halt on March 31, Butchko was very popular.

After Johnson stopped bombing most of Vietnam, and withdrew from the Presidential race on March 31, the Burbank Daily Review interviewed Butchko and stated: "John T. Butchko, Democratic candidate in the 27th Congressional District, said he has felt that the President would withdraw."

"I was most surprised at the timing. I thought that if he did withdraw it would come after the primaries, particularly the California primary".

"The local resident termed the President's decision to stop the bombing 'a move in the right direction."

"Butchko said he has supported the candidacy of Eugene McCarthy for the Democratic nomination as the party's 'most qualified man' and he added, that he would continue to support McCarthy."

In early April, the Valley Green Sheet published a list of the members of Butchko's campaign committee, and stated that Butchko has called for immediate cessation of the bombing of North Vietnam as the first towards negotiations to end the war.

In early April of 1968, Butchko spoke at a candidate's forum sponsored by the American Legion at a restaurant in Van Nuys. An article in the Valley Green Sheet, based on Butchko's press release, announced that Butchko would speak at this event. Butchko gave his full speech on Vietnam at this forum. Jim Miller in the course of his speech, said, "I do not agree with John Butchko."

In 1968, a Russian-American name such as John Butchko was the best kind of name a candidate could have.

In 1968, all of the members of Johnson's cabinet were Anglo-Saxons.

An article in the Newhall Signal in March stated that Butchko would appear at a gathering of Democrats in Val Verde.

On April 3, Martin Luther King, Jr., was assassinated.

On the evening of April 3, Butchko appeared at a special meeting of the Burbank Human Relations council and said that fair housing was important.

Shortly after the assassination of Martin Luther King, Jr., there were riots in many major cities in the United States. Similar riots in the early summer of 1967 had not caused a de-escalation of the War in Vietnam.

Shortly after the assassination of Martin Luther King, Jr., Congress passed a fair housing bill. Reinecke voted against it. An article published in the Newhall Signal criticized Reinecke for voting against the fair housing bill and pointed out that most Republicans had voted for it.

In early April of 1968, Butchko spoke at a candidate's forum sponsored by the Independent Young Democratic Club at the Unitarian "Onion" Church Hall in the West Valley. Mary Bockwinkel, the President of the Independent Young Democratic Club, introduced Butchko and said that: "Butchko is our favorite candidate." In the course of his speech, Butchko called for the establishment of all volunteer armed forces, and elimination of the draft.

In early April of 1968, Butchko spoke at a dinner of the Burbank Human Relations Council. He attacked Reinecke as a hawk. Doris Straus, an activist in the Council, said that Butchko had scored some points by his speech.

In April, Butchko appeared at a meeting of the Sunland-Tujunga Democratic Club.

In April Butchko spoke at the grand opening of the headquarters of the Sunland Tujunga Democratic Club in Sunland. An article was published in the Record Ledger along with Butchko's picture at the headquarter's opening. This article described Butchko's appearance at the headquarter's opening.

In early April of 1968, McCarthy won the Wisconsin primary over Lyndon Johnson by a margin of four to three or three to two. Johnson had withdrawn from the race too late to take his name off the ballot.

In 1968, there were far fewer presidential primaries than in subsequent years.

In 1968, the voting age was twenty-one.

In April, the Lockheed Machinists Union invited Butchko to appear at a special interview at the Machinists Hall in Burbank. Butchko was well received. He was subsequently endorsed by the Machinists Union. An article was than published in the Burbank Daily Review stating that Butchko had been endorsed for Congress by the International Association of Machinists. This article stated Butchko's position on several issues and said that he favored a guaranteed minimum income, including incentives to work.

On January 8, 1968, the Newhall Signal published an article based on an exclusive interview with Reinecke in which the Congressman said he was shocked to learn about the recent arrest of Edgar Eugene Bradley of North Hollywood, a west coast representative for radio evangelist Carl McIntyre and a former member of the Burbank Auxiliary Police. Jim Garrison had arranged for the arrest of Bradley in California, and Garrison was seeking to have Bradley extradited to New Orleans to face prosecution on charges of involvement in a conspiracy to assassinate John F. Kennedy. Reinecke said about Bradley, "I realized I knew him from some place. I had met him once or twice. I knew that." Bradley told the Signal that he had been a campaign supporter of Reinecke, but he added, "I probably know him better than he knows me." The Signal stated that Bradley indicated that he had played an active role in Reinecke's past campaigns, and that he said he planned to get in touch with Reinecke as soon as he could. Butchko discussed these news items with Travers in Butchko's office.

On April 17, 1968, Bradley and Reinecke were feature speakers at a luncheon meeting of the Sunland-Tujunga Republican Women's Club. Butchko discussed these news items with Travers in Butchko's office.

Reinecke resided in North Hollywood.

In May, Loren Hall, a Kernville bartender whom Garrison was seeking to extradite as a witness for his forthcoming New Orleans trial, stated that he had stood next to Bradley while a conversation was being carried out about the possibility of assassinating John F. Kennedy. Hall said the conversation was just a few weeks before the assassination and the occasion was just after Hall had delivered a speech at a house in Los Angeles. Hall had been involved in anti-Castro activities in Miami, New Orleans and Dallas. Bradley stated that he had not been in the house on the occasion of Hall's speech, but had been there on a different date and occasion to listen to a speech by a former FBI agent and that Colonel William P. Gale was present in the audience on that occasion. Butchko and Travers discussed these news items in Butchko's office.

Governor Reagan's decision on Bradley's extradition to Louisiana was not handed down until early 1969. Bradley was not extradited.

In April of 1968, at a meeting of the Democratic Women's League of the San Fernando Valley, Corman stated, when asked whom he was supporting for President, that he had supported Lyndon Johnson. Butchko also spoke at this meeting and stated his support for McCarthy. An article in the Valley Green Sheet announced this meeting and stated that Butchko and other candidates would speak at it.

In April, the McCarthy peace slate campaign of the Sixty-Fourth Assembly District Democratic Council conducted a motorcade throughout the West Valley.

60

Butchko rode in the motorcade in an open car, and Gary Ramer, the California Democratic Council endorsed candidate for Assembly also rode in the motorcade along with members of the Sixty-Fourth Assembly District Democratic Council. The cars in the motorcade had signs for McCarthy, Bielenson, Butchko and Ramer attached to them. The Los Angeles Times, San Fernando Valley section, published an article stating when and where the motorcade would take place and stating that Butchko would ride in it. This article clearly indicated that Butchko was supporting McCarthy.

In April when McCarthy arrived at the Burbank Airport to a large crowd, members of the Independent Young Democratic Club displayed Butchko's quartercards on poles. Butchko appeared at a gathering for McCarthy at a hall in Los Angeles.

Jerry Brown there told Chuck Jacobsen, a friend of Butchko's, that Butchko was a "leftist." Butchko's friend replied to Jerry Brown that, "Butchko is a good man," and that he was supporting Butchko. Butchko spoke with people at this gathering.

At the very large outdoor rally for McCarthy on the campus of San Fernando Valley State College in Northridge in about April, Butchko sat on the platform along with McCarthy and Mildred Simon, and Butchko was formally introduced before a large portion of the student body as "the Democratic candidate for Congress in the Twenty-Seventh Congressional District and a candidate supporting McCarthy." At this rally, Butchko received huge applause from a huge crowd. This crowd consisted of 8,000 people.

During the 1968 primary election campaign, Jeanne Caya, an active supporter of Butchko, was placed in charge of the main McCarthy Headquarters in San Franando Valley. Jeanne Caya had proposed Butchko for endorsement at the March convention of

61

the Twenty-Seventh congressional District Democratic Council. Butchko had his campaign cards in this headquarters.

In April, Butchko appeared at a heavily attended meeting of the Valley Peace Slate Steering Committee for McCarthy at a school in the Valley, at which Ben Leeds introduced Butchko as the Honorable John T. Butchko, the Democratic candidate for Congress in the Twenty-Seventh Congressional District. At Ben Leed's request, Butchko led the salute to the flag. In speaking at this meeting, Butchko pointed out that Butchko was now the virtual Democratic nominee for Congress since the time for filing had expired and Butchko was unopposed in the Democratic primary. Butchko said that he was firmly supporting McCarthy now, and that he hoped and trusted that these eager McCarthy supporters would remember him in the general election campaign.

In about April, Reagan said that the nation was "out of control." This statement was hyperbole.

In early April of 1968, Butchko spoke at a meeting of the Sherman Oaks Democratic Club at a Hall in Studio City. Butchko gave his full speech on Vietnam at this meeting. An article in the Valley Green Sheet, announcing that Butchko would gave this speech, described Butchko's background and stated that it was expected that Butchko would call for immediate cessation of the bombing of North Vietnam as a first step toward negotiations to end the war. An article in the Glendale Independent also announced the speech in an article that described Butchko's background. After Butchko's speech, Ben Renaldo's brother told Travers that Butchko would be an exciting candidate. Ben Renaldo was the Chairman of the Twenty-Seventh Congressional District Democratic Council.

In May of 1968, the Valley Green Sheet published an article, which stated:

"John T. Butchko today announced the appointment of Ted Lane, Canoga Park, and Charles, Paioni, Northridge to his campaign committee."

"Butchko is the Democratic candidate for Congress in the 27th District."

"An attorney in Burbank and an elected member of the Los Angeles County Democratic Central Committee, he is unopposed in the Democratic primary."

"Lane is the President of the Reseda-West Valley Democratic Club and has long been active in the work of Democratic Clubs in the West Valley. He has praised Butchko's programs for preservation of the family farm as part of our way of life."

"Paioni is an architect and a member of the Granada Hills Democratic Club."

In April or May of 1968, the Valley Green Sheet published an article stating:

"John T. Butchko, the Democratic candidate for congress in the 27th Congressional District, had stated today that, if elected, he would seek the enactment of legislation to provide for a limited number of free mailings for party candidates for national office."

"Butchko said that such a provision would be fairer and would result in better representation than the present method which allows the incumbents only to have a virtually unlimited number of free mailings."

"Butchko is an attorney in Burbank and an elected member of the Los Angeles County Democratic Central Committee. He is unopposed in the Democratic primary."

In April or May, Butchko received a letter from Californians for Liberal Representation stating that that organization supported him. The Newhall Signal soon published an article stating that Butchko had been endorsed by Californians for Liberal Representation. Arthur Carstens was the President of Californians for Liberal Representation.

In April or May of 1968, Butchko spoke at a candidate's forum of North Hollywood Adult School at North Hollywood High School, and afterwards drove to Van Nuys where he spoke to the Van Nuys Democratic Club. An article in the Glendale Independent announced that Butchko would speak at the candidate's forum of the North Hollywood Adult School. An article in the Valley Green Sheet announced that Butchko would speak at this meeting of the Van Nuys Democratic Club, and stated his position on several issues.

In April or May, Butchko spoke at a political candidates fair sponsored by the League of Women Voters in Encino. An article in the Valley Green Sheet announced that Butchko would speak at this event. This article said: "Literature describing the candidacy of John T. Butchko will be distributed at the event, which is a political candidate's fair."

" Butchko is an attorney in Burbank and a member of the Los Angeles County Democratic Central Committee."

Throughout the 1968 election, both before and after the primary, the Valley Green Sheet announced Butchko's forthcoming speeches in the San Fernando Valley when there was enough time to get the press releases regarding the speech to the Valley Green Sheet in advance of the speech.

On a Saturday in May of 1968, someone drove Travers around the Antelope Valley in a truck, from which Travers passed out Butchko's campaign cards to a large number of people there. Travers told Butchko that this venture was very successful.

In the May 27, 1968 edition of the Los Angeles Herald Examiner, an article listed some of the Congressional candidates in Los Angeles County and said regarding the Twenty-Seventh Congressional District: "Congressman Reinecke, a Republican, faces conservative William P. Gale of Saugus and Jim Miller in the GOP primary. John T. Butchko, Burbank lawyer, is the only Democrat running." In April Butchko appeared, and spoke and answered questions at a meeting of the interviewing committee of the Jeanette Rankin Brigade in downtown Los Angeles. Butchko was well received.

In many of Butchko's 1968 speeches after March 31, he called for immediate and complete cessation of all bombing of North Vietnam, and in some of these speeches he attacked Reinecke as a hawk.

Butchko found a vacant store on the mall in downtown Burbank for the Burbank McCarthy headquarters.

During 1968, some of the articles in the Valley Green Sheet announcing Butchko's forthcoming speeches also stated his position on some issues, and before June of 1968, some of them stated that he was an elected member of the Los Angeles County Democratic Central Committee.

In April, during the primary campaign, Butchko spoke at the formal opening of the Burbank McCarthy headquarters on the Golden Mall in downtown Burbank. An article in the Burbank Daily Review announced that Butchko would speak at this event. This headquarters operation was run by a lady who was very friendly to Butchko. From this headquarters, some campaign workers delivered to many residences in Burbank, Butchko's campaign cards and a campaign piece that Butchko used for the primary. This campaign piece had his picture and a statement of his background and his position on several issues including a statement that he had stated that a peacetime economy will provide new opportunities for tax reductions and increased business growth. Butchko also placed a large stack of these campaign pieces in the headquarters of the Sunland-Tujunga Democratic Club from which they were delivered to residences in that area.

Ever since he announced his candidacy for the Democratic nomination for President, in about April of 1968, Hubert Humphrey had more delegates than any other candidate.

In May, Butchko spoke at a candidate's forum sponsored by the West Valley Jewish Community Center in Canoga Park. An article in the Valley Green Sheet announced that Butchko would speak at this event and stated Butchko's position on several issues. Reinecke also spoke there but Reinecke appeared confused and said that he favored returning the conquered territories to Israel. Right after this speech, Butchko drove to a party sponsored by the Northwest Valley Democratic Club. Butchko also spoke at this party and attacked Reinecke on the civil rights issues. After this speech, Robert Marks, a member of the Independent Young Democratic Club of the San Fernando Valley complimented Butchko on the quality of his speeches and especially that speech.

In May, Butchko spoke at a candidate's forum sponsored by a business and professional women's club in the South Valley. In this speech, Butchko attacked Reinecke on civil rights issues.

In May, Reinecke mailed to everyone in the Twenty-Seventh Congressional District a report from Washington using his franking privilege a piece which said that Johnson had undertaken a military adventure which had cost the United States a heavy price in blood and treasure. Butchko's press release was published in the Newhall Saugus Sun and Sylmar Breeze, describing Reinecke's statement and saying that no administration would be able to undertake a military adventure if it were not for incumbents like Reinecke who call for escalation.

In May, Butchko had a booth for one week on the grounds of San Fernando State College as a part of the college's candidates program. Butchko's campaign signs were attached to his booth and volunteers passed out Butchko's campaign cards and campaign piece at the booth all week. As a part of the program, Butchko spoke to a good sized audience on the grounds of the campus. Articles were published in the Valley Green Sheet and in the Northridger announcing that Butchko would speak at this event and that it was expected that Butchko would call for immediate cessation of the bombing of North Vietnam as a first step toward negotiations to end the war.

Throughout 1968 before the general election, Butchko attended all of the meetings of the Twenty-Seventh Congressional District Democratic Council, many meetings of the Fifty-Seventh Assembly District Democratic Council and the Sixty-Fourth Assembly District Democratic Council, and many meetings and parties of the California Democratic Clubs affiliated with the Twenty-Seventh Congressional District Democratic Council. Butchko delivered a speech or spoke with people at these meetings and parties.

In 1968, there were about 500 members of the California Democratic Clubs living in the Twenty-Seventh Congressional District, and so Butchko could count on at least 500 campaign workers to walk precincts.

Until the middle of July, the Los Angeles Times, San Fernando Valley Section, announced that Butchko would give some of his speeches that he gave. The San Gabriel Valley Section of the Los Angeles Times also published some publicity announcing Butchko's speeches.

In May of 1968, Butchko received a typewritten letter from a man in Ohio, whom he did not know. In this letter this man said that he and his friends were "hoping" for a Butchko election victory.

Before the primary election, precinct workers working from the Sixty-Fourth Assembly District Democratic Council's headquarters on Sherman Way in Canoga Park distributed that Council's slate piece, which listed their endorsed candidates, including McCarthy for President, Bill Morosoff for State Senate, Anthony Bielenson for United States Senate, John T. Butchko for Congress in the Twenty-Seventh Congressional District, and Guy Raner for State Assembly, to the residences of most of the registered Democrats in that Assembly District. Along with that slate piece, many of them also distributed Butchko's campaign cards and the campaign piece he was using for the primary. The slate piece was mailed to those precincts, which were not reached by campaign walkers, who delivered the slate piece and Butchko's literature.

The Fifty-Seventh Assembly District Democratic Council mailed their slate piece to every registered Democrat in that Assembly District. In the Studio City, Sherman Oaks, and other Twenty-Seventh Congressional District portions of the Fifty-

Seventh Assembly District, their slate piece listed John T. Butchko as their endorsed candidate in the Twenty-Seventh Congressional District. Precinct walkers, working in that council's headquarters on Van Nuys Boulevard in Sherman Oaks, also distributed individual campaign pieces of their endorsed candidates, including a stack of Butchko's campaign cards and campaign piece used in the primary campaign, to a substantial number of precincts. The other portions of the Twenty-Seventh Congressional District situated in the Fifty-Seventh Assembly District included Toluca Lake, part of North Hollywood, that part of Burbank south of Oak Street and some other areas. These portions of the Twenty-Seventh Congressional District also received in the mail the slate piece of the Fifty-Seventh Assembly District Democratic Council endorsing McCarthy for President, Anthony Bielenson for United States Senate, John T. Butchko for Congress, William Morosoff for State Senate and Dorothy Bereny for State Assembly.

On a Saturday in May, shortly before the June primary, Butchko and Travers drove to Bakersfield for a television appearance by Butchko at a large park in Bakersfield. On the way to Bakersfield, they stopped at a gas station in Gorman and spoke with the gentleman in charge of the station. Butchko gave him a stack of his campaign cards and he said that he would pass them out.

All the candidates on the ballot in Kern County spoke on KERO-TV at this park in Bakersfield. Butchko started his speech by saying, "I have called for de-escalation and negotiations to end the war in Vietnam." The audience of 200 people then interrupted Butchko's speech with applause. Butchko was the only candidate whose speech was interrupted by applause. Right after Butchko spoke, William Gayle spoke and said that "Democrats like the one who just spoke, are selling out the country." Reinecke had

69

arranged to have his speech presented by videotape. After their speeches, an employee of KERO-TV told Butchko that Butchko had come over good on television. Travers told Butchko that he had come over better than Reinecke on television.

Shortly before the primary election there were published candidates pages in the Valley Green Sheet, the Los Angeles Times, San Fernando Valley edition and the Burbank Daily Review. All of these candidates' pages published a statement of Butchko's background, and a statement of his views, including a statement that he favored immediate cessation of the bombing of North Vietnam. The candidate's pages in the Valley Green Sheet and the Burbank Daily Review also published Butchko's picture. In the candidate's page in the Los Angeles Times, San Fernando Valley edition, Reinecke called for a firm commitment to the military effort. In most of the candidates pages Reinecke said he favored an honorable peace. By this he meant a military victory.

In the edition preceding the June primary, the American Aeronaut, the official newspaper of the Lockheed Machinists Union, there was published an article stating that Butchko was the endorsed candidate of the Machinists Union, including his picture and a statement that he favored increasing the personal exemption for federal income taxes to at least $1,000.00. The article stated that Butchko was a Democrat. The same article was published in the edition of the American Aeronaut immediately preceding the general election. This newspaper was mailed to well over 15,000 residences.

Shortly before the primary, Butchko met with Tom Carrell, who said Butchko might win the general election.

Shortly before the June primary, the Newhall Signal published an editorial stating that Reinecke was unfit to be a Congressman, but that Butchko had been clear on the war in Vietnam and that "he was a young man to watch."

Shortly before the primary, the Newhall Signal published an editorial on the Twenty-Seventh Congressional District race.

This editorial stated in part: "The second contest for national office presents us with a sad date of affairs as far as Republicans go. Three men are vying as candidates for the Congress race from the Twenty- Seventh District – Jim Miller, William Gale and incumbent Edwin Reinecke. We have no real respect for any of them."

"Mr. Miller has consistently voiced himself as a preacher against Communism. His role has that of a negativist and reactionary, and his beliefs about the so-called Communist menace indicate that he is not capable of responsible political thought."

"We have the same opinion of William Gale, with the added note that he would probably be a more dangerous man if he were elected, then would be Miller."

"As for congressman Reinecke, though we have endorsed him in the past in both primary and general elections, we have changed our opinion considerably this year. We felt, during previous endorsements, that Mr. Reinecke showed great promise. He has, however, not lived up to the hopes we had for him. In fact, he has not lived up to much as a Congressman."

"In the final analysis, we have discovered that Congressman Edwin Reinecke is not deserving of the sacred trust of the public. He is a man who seems to be almost devoid of human compassion, or the ability to understand modern society. We regard these qualities, which Mr. Reinecke so clearly lacks, as essential in fulfilling the role as a

71

member of the House of Representatives. We cannot, in good conscience, offer an endorsement of any of the Republicans running for Congress.

"In the Democratic ranks, there is perhaps some hope. John T. Butchko is running unopposed as a Democrat; Butchko has not been extremely vocal in his campaign yet, because he is waiting, obviously, to campaign against the Republican winner. However, Butchko has been very clear on the military effort in Vietnam. We believe that this is a healthy attitude. Butchko is most likely a young man to watch."

When the June 4 votes were counted, Butchko received 53,996 votes, including the Kern County vote. Reinecke received 66,318 votes. Jim Miller received 4,502 votes. William Gale received 3,692 votes.

McCarthy carried Butchko's district by more than 10,000 votes over Kennedy, and McCarthy carried every major portion of the district. Butchko had permitted Travers to devote considerable time to press work for the McCarthy campaign and the coordinated California Democratic Council campaigns in the district.

Shortly after the primary, Jeanne Caya told Butchko that the Twenty-Seventh Congressional District had been McCarthy's second best district in the State of California. Hubert Humphrey's name was not on the ballot in the California primary.

By any objective standard, Butchko now had to be regarded as one of the top leaders of the peace movement in California in view of a combination of facts: (1) he had consistently since March of 1967, opposed the renomination of Lyndon Johnson; (2) he had received tremendous amounts of publicity in the San Fernando Valley and in the Twenty-Seventh Congressional District identifying himself with the proposition that all bombing of North Vietnam should be immediately terminated, and 3) while doing these

72

things, he had become the unopposed Democratic Candidate for Congress in a district where a Democrat had a chance to win, and he had received a high vote in the June primary.

Although Butchko had hoped to get more votes than Reinecke in the primary, a careful study of the returns showed that he had received a very high vote for a Democrat in this district. Butchko had received more votes than the combined votes of all the candidates for the Democratic nomination for Congress in the former Twenty-Seventh Congressional District in the 1966 primary. Reinecke had abundant publicity and mailers during that time. Reinecke's name had been known for years and especially since 1964. Reinecke had received more than 6,000 Democratic write-in votes in the 1966 primary. This time the ballot did not provide a space for write-in votes, and they could only be indicated by a voter's writing in the name of the office and the candidate, and they could be tabulated only if the candidate had filed as a write-in candidate. Reinecke had not done so.

Butchko's campaign expenditures before the primary had been approximately $2,500, a remarkably small sum for 53,996 votes. He had received only $150 in campaign contributions. It seemed reasonable to expect that with adequate financing, Butchko could make up the difference and win in November.

Right after the primary, the Hollywood Citizen-News published Butchko's picture and, Reinecke's picture as the winners of their primaries, and an article describing an interview with Butchko, which quoted Butchko as stating that he intended to conduct an aggressive campaign on the issues and to bring out the incumbent's voting record. That article was entitled: "Butchko face off with Reinecke."

73

Right after the primary the Valley Green Sheet published pictures of Reinecke and Butchko and stated that Reinecke had easily won the Republican primary and was opposed by John T. Butchko, a Democrat.

Right after the primary the San Fernando Valley Times published an article entitled: "Butchko Face Off With Reinecke." This article stated that John T. Butchko was unopposed in the Democratic primary and that Butchko said the situation in Vietnam is the main issue and that Butchko promised to campaign hard.

After the primary, the Daily Ledger Gazette in the Antelope Valley and the Glendale Independent both published individual articles describing the primary election results in the Twenty-Seventh Congressional District.

In June after the primary, Butchko appeared at a meeting of a California Democratic Council unit at Valley City College in Van Nuys. At this meeting a man from the Newhall-Saugus area said to the entire group that he wanted to work for Butchko. Butchko spoke with some people at this meeting, and he told Lesley Chambers that he wanted to have a mailer.

Shortly after the primary, Butchko received a letter advertising the service of Hal Avery's public relations firm. Butchko called Avery and asked him if he did fundraising. He did not, but Avery said that he had analyzed the district and the primary election vote and had concluded that Butchko could win. He said that he did not know what Butchko had done to get the high vote he did, but he said that the Republican National Committee was now worried about losing this Congressional seat.

After the shocking assassination of Robert F. Kennedy on the night of his victory in the California primary, Butchko observed a moratorium of several weeks in respect to campaigning. Reinecke mailed a "Report from Washington" to all the voters in the district in June. He got some publicity in district newspapers for press releases stating that he opposed any entry into the United States of "Red" Rudi Dutchke, a German student radical leader. Reinecke felt that that was a timely publicity feature.

Butchko communicated with State Senator Tom Carrell regarding receiving Tom's endorsement in June. In a telephone conversation, Tom Carrell assured Butchko that he had mailed a press release declaring his endorsement of Butchko to a newspaper in the north San Fernando Valley.

In June, the Valley Green Sheet published an article stating that Butchko would appear and speak at a meeting of the Sixty-Fourth Assembly District Democratic Council at the Council's headquarters on Sherman Way in Canoga Park.

This article stated: "Butchko is an attorney in Burbank. He is running on a platform of peace in Vietnam, against incumbent Edwin Reinecke."

"Butchko has called for immediate cessation of all bombing in North Vietnam and negotiations with all parties to end the war in Vietnam as soon as possible."

In this speech to the Sixty-Fourth Assembly District Democratic Council, Butchko said that the most effective way they could now help the McCarthy campaign was by vigorously supporting the local candidates who were supporting McCarthy.

The next week Butchko spoke at a meeting of a California Democratic Council unit in the Fifty-Seventh Assembly District. An article in the Valley Green Sheet announced that Butchko would give this speech.

In June, Butchko visited the office of the Northridger newspaper. The editor told Butchko that she had been publishing his press releases and showed him a recent

75

back issue of the Northridger containing an article announcing one of Butchko's speeches and stating that it was expected that Butchko would call for immediate cessation of the bombing of North Vietnam. She told Butchko "Whether you win or lose, you will win."

In June, Butchko challenged Reinecke to a debate in a letter sent by registered mail. The Valley Green Sheet, the Burbank Daily Review, the North Valley Mail and Reseda Post, and another newspaper delivered to in the Newhall, Saugus and Valencia area published the article describing Butchko's challenge to Reinecke to debate and stating that Butchko had said that the voters are entitled to know the difference between the candidates. When there was no early response from Reinecke, Butchko renewed his challenge, and he got some more publicity for that in an article published in the Valley Green Sheet. Reinecke was thus pushed into a reply on Friday, July 5, a registered letter from the Congressman was delivered to Butchko in which the Congressman seemed to agree in principle with the concept of a debate but added: "Recognizing, of course that Congress is now in session, and that it is rather indefinite as to when I will be in California, I cannot give a firm answer at this time, but I trust that any two offices will be able to get together in order to make such a meeting possible." The answer was not very straightforward. Reinecke had returned to the district for campaign activities during the week of the July 4, Independence Day holiday. When Butchko received the letter, Reinecke was in the District. The Newhall Signal published an article that pointed that out The Valley Green Sheet published Reinecke's reply in publishing a press release sent out by Butchko, and stating that Butchko said that Reinecke had answered thus.

After the primary, Travers resigned as Butchko's campaign manager to get a job where he could earn more money.

In June of 1968 Butchko and Jeanne Caya were invited to dinner at the home of a wealthy Democrat in Granada Hills. At this event , Jeanne Caya said that Butchko had the best grasp of the issues of any candidate she had seen.

In early July, the Valley Green Sheet published an article stating that Butchko favored extending the protection of the national labor laws to farm workers.

In early July the Valley Green Sheet published an article stating that:

"John T. Butchko, the Democratic candidate for Congress in the 27th Congressional District had stated today that he favors federal legislation requiring major television stations to give free and equal time to party candidates for national office.'

"Butchko said that in Los Angeles County, where there are approximately 16 Congressional districts, a program giving five minutes to each of four candidates in each of the districts would take a total of 320 minutes, or less than six hours.'

"The total would be reduced by reason of the fact that in some districts there are only two candidates."

"Butchko said that this kind of program is the best way to acquaint voters with their candidates for Congress. This kind of program has been presented on KERO television in Bakersfield, where all the candidates on the ballot in Kern County in a recent election were invited to appear."

"Butchko said that the basis for legislation requiring major television stations assume this responsibility is the fact that the airwaves are public property which television stations are licensed to use."

In the first part of July the Valley Green Sheet published an article stating that Butchko had charged that Reinecke was absent on 103 out of 193 yea-nay roll-call votes

77

in the 1966 session of the 89th Congress, and that on 22 of the 103 absences Reinecke was paired with another either for or against a measure but that on 81 of the roll-calls Reinecke was not even paired. The article also stated that Butchko stated that the Twenty-Seventh Congressional District needs and deserves full-time representation in Congress.

After Travers resigned, Butchko had to conduct a Congressional campaign in a district of over 4,000 square miles and over 600,000 people with no paid workers. As a Congressman, Reinecke had several employees paid by the federal government. The financial strain was becoming enormous. Butchko had to be constantly on the offensive to unseat an incumbent with five years of cumulative publicity.

Butchko sought unsuccessfully to raise funds. He sought to find a fundraiser.

Butchko had hoped to get some money from labor. It seemed likely that he would be endorsed by the AFL-CIO for the general election because he had already got the endorsement of the conservative Machinists Union, and because it would look unusual for his name to be omitted from the slate of endorsed candidates, which COPE, would publish and distribute throughout the County before the election.

Butchko noted that labor groups were already holding fund raising parties for Alan Cranston, Jim Corman and other COPE endorsed candidates. Butchko was being left out because of the COPE refusal to endorse him before the primary. Butchko was especially displeased when Mary Dermody told him that Reinecke and other Republican candidates spoke at a certain July 4 public gathering in the Antelope Valley and that the emcee had stated that all the other candidates had been invited and did not care to come. Butchko had received no invitation or information concerning the event.

78

Butchko asked several television and radio interview programs for an opportunity to speak. His requests were declined. Reasons given are that the programs did not permit candidates to speak because equal time would have to be given to all other candidates. However, Joe Holt, the winning candidate for the Republican nomination for Congress in the Twenty-Second Congressional District had been permitted to appear on a television program of this type during the primary campaign, while his opponents did not appear. Butchko pointed out that the only other candidate who might be entitled to equal time was Reinecke since there were no major party candidates for Congress in the district. But it was to no avail.

Butchko felt in July that he had been unfairly discriminated against by the leaders of organized labor who had a say in the decision not to endorse him before the primary. He thought it was unusual that he got almost no contributions at all although he himself had personally mounted a strong campaign.

In June, he had written to Jess Unruh asking for a campaign contribution, but he received no reply from Unruh.

In the middle of July Butchko met with the Kern County leaders of the AFL-CIO in Bakersfield and answered their questions, and afterward he went to a meeting of the Kern County Democratic Central Committee in Bakersfield where he was introduced as the Democratic nominee for Congress in the Twenty-Seventh District. The members of that Central Committee discussed ways of aiding Butchko's campaign.

In spite of the financial difficulties it still appeared to Butchko and to his friends that he still had a good chance to win. But the tide of the campaign turned abruptly in favor of Reinecke on about July 22. It then became obvious to Butchko that the Masons had united against his campaign. This was the first time that the Masons had united against a candidate who had already gone so far.

When this happened, Alan Cranston, the Democratic nominee for U.S. Senate, called for a halt to the bombing of North Vietnam. Before July 22, Alan Cranston had never called for such a bombing halt. It makes sense to figure that the Masons had made Alan Cranston co-opt the most significant position on the issues with which Butchko was identified. Butchko continued to slug it out with Reineke.

In late July or very early August the Newhall Signal published an article stating that Butchko favored lowering the voting age to 18.

At about the same time the Valley Green Sheet published an article stating:

"John T. Butchko, the Democratic candidate for Congress in the Twenty-Seventh Congressional District had stated today that he favors lowering the voting age to 18."

"Butchko, an attorney in Burbank, has proposed numerous electoral reforms, including:

1. – A nationwide presidential primary.

2. – Better criteria for the determination of election districts.

3. – Limited tax credits for contributions to political candidates."

Early in August, the Valley Green Sheet published Butchko's press release announcing that a Meet the Candidate's Day for John T. Butchko would be held at the headquarters of the Sixty-Fourth Assembly District Democratic Council on Sherman Way in Canoga Park on a certain Saturday. At this Meet the Candidate's Day, a member of the Independent Young Democratic Club of the San Fernando Valley told Butchko that he thought that Butchko would carry Chatsworth.

This recent publicity regained some momentum for Butchko's campaign.

In early August Butchko spoke to an interviewing committee of ADA in downtown Los Angeles. He was soon informed of his endorsement by the ADA (Americans for Democratic Action).

In early August, Butchko spoke at a very large meeting of Democrats in a hall at Los Angeles Valley City College in Van Nuys. Lorry Sherman and Mildred Simon also spoke there, and they saw and heard Butchko speak. Butchko made a strong speech contrasting himself with Reinecke and attacking Reinecke as a hawk.

In early August the Valley Green Sheet published an article (Butchko's press release) stating that Butchko had been appointed to the Credentials Committee of the meeting of the Democratic State Central Committee to be held in Sacramento in August. Butchko had been appointed to the post by Charles Warren, the State Chairman of the Democratic Party.

In the first part of August the Valley Green Sheet published Butchko's press release stating that Butchko had been endorsed by Americans for Democratic Action, and that Butchko said: "American for Democratic Action is a young organization on the scale of history; but in its desire for excellence, it is as old as the impulse which gave this nation birth."

In August of 1968, the Valley Green Sheet, the Reminder and the San Fernando Valley Sun all published a blockbuster press release of Butchko stating that: In the Congressional Record, Reinecke had criticized the expression by the Johnson

Administration of a willingness to negotiate an end to the war in Vietnam on the grounds that it could be interpreted as a weakening of our national resolve. This article began by stating that Butchko stated that Reinecke had said this.

Butchko's sending his press releases to many, many newspapers, radio stations and other media had a tremendous impact on advancing the peace movement.

In about the middle of August, the Valley Green Sheet published Butchko's press release stating that Jack Howard endorsed Butchko for Congress in the Twenty-Seventh Congressional District. This article described Jack Howard's background and stated that Jack Howard was a member of the Robert Kennedy delegation to the Democratic national convention, and that Jack Howard had been the Democratic nominee for Congress in the former Twenty-Seventh Congressional District in 1966.

On the Sunday of the meeting of the Democratic State Central Committee, the Valley Green Sheet published a Butchko press release stating that Butchko would speak at a meeting of a California Democratic Council unit in Sherman Oaks, and that it was expected that Butchko would call for immediate cessation of the bombing of North Vietnam as a first step toward negotiations to end the war in Vietnam.

At the meeting of the Democratic State Central Committee in Sacramento in August, Butchko sought to be elected a member of the Executive Board of the Democratic State Central Committee. A caucus of the Twenty-Seventh District members met on Saturday night. Norbert Schlei, who had been a Democratic nominee for Secretary of State was in the caucus. Leonard Maizlich, the Democratic nominee for Assembly in the Fifty-Seventh Assembly District, told Butchko to make some friends. On Saturday evening, Ted Lane spoke on behalf of Butchko and said simply that Butchko was the Democratic candidate for Congress in the Twenty-Seventh Congressional District. Butchko was defeated by Dan Axelrod, who had run in 1966 as a Jess Unruh backed Democrat against a California Democratic Council endorsed candidate in the primary in the Fifty-Seventh Assembly District. In September John Dermody, Mary Dermody's husband, told Butchko that he did not understand why things happened the way they did at that caucus.

On the Sunday before the Republican National Convention, Butchko appeared at a party at the home of a California Democratic Council Club member in the West Valley, and he spoke with some people there.

Shortly after Butchko returned to Burbank from Sacramento, He met with Clyde Bullock, the President of the United Auto Workers in Van Nuys. Clyde Bullock informed Butchko that he had been endorsed by the Los Angeles County Federation of Labor AFL-CIO. This was in the latter part of August. On this occasion, Clyde Bullock said that Butchko's heavy publicity in the Valley Green Sheet was unusual for a Democratic candidate. He also said that the AFL-CIO's failure to endorse Butchko before the primary did not make sense.

In August of 1968 after a 12:15 Mass at Saint Finnbar Church in Burbank where Butchko was an usher, Butchko was invited by Fred Kubasak to his home in Burbank. Fred Kubasak was the owner of the Valley Funeral Home in Burbank and an active member of the Knights of Columbus in Burbank. At Mr. Kubasak's home in the backyard, Butchko discussed politics with Fred Kubasak and his friends. Fred Kubasak then gave Butchko Everett Burkhalter's telephone number. In late August, Butchko called Everett Burkhalter and was invited to his home on a Saturday in September.

In late August Butchko spoke at a meeting of a California Democratic Council unit in a large backyard of a home in Sherman Oaks, where he attacked Reinecke as a hawk as hard as he could.

Also in late August, the Valley Green Sheet published Butchko's press release announcing that Butchko would appear at the Antelope Valley Fair in Lancaster, and stating three of Butchko's views, including a statement that Butchko favored a repeal of the 10% surcharge on income taxes.

Before the Antelope Valley Fair, Butchko visited Mary Dermody, the Democratic nominee for Assembly at her home in Lancaster, and gave her a large quantity of Butchko's campaign matchbooks for distribution at the Democratic booth at the Fair. Mary Dermody said that Butchko would look better than Reinecke at the Antelope Valley Fair. Mary Dermody liked Butchko's matchbooks. On the inside of these matchbooks, there was a summary of Butchko's background similar to the description of his background on his campaign cards. He also gave Mary Dermody a large quantity of his campaign cards for distribution at the Fair.

Shortly before the national Democratic Convention the Soviet Union invaded Czechoslovakia. This was a setback for Butchko's campaign and for other Democratic candidates for national office.

The Democratic convention in Chicago resembled a brawl, and it therefore appeared that the nominee, Hubert Humphrey, had no chance to win in the general election.

Butchko appeared at Antelope Valley Fair for the first two days of the Fair. There he passed out his literature, campaign cards, and talked with many people at the

Democratic booth. He talked with Harold Greenberg, who was then an attorney in the Antelope Valley. Butchko sat in the grandstand where the outdoor activities, some rodeo-like, took place and he was introduced as the Democratic nominee for Congress on both days.

On Labor Day, the next day, Butchko appeared and spoke at a large Labor Day picnic of the AFL-CIO at a large park in Sylmar. Butchko there attacked Reinecke for his absentee voting record. Butchko exchanged greetings with Alan Cranston, and with Cesar Chavez, to whom he gave his campaign card. Butchko spoke individually with many people there and passed out his campaign cards.

In September, the Daily Ledger Gazette published at least one of Butchko's press releases every week. The Daily Ledger Gazette was in the Antelope Valley.

Shortly after the Democratic convention, the Valley Green Sheet published an article stating: "John T. Butchko, the Democratic candidate for Congress in the Twenty-Seventh Congressional District, today had stated that he dissents from the platform planks on Vietnam adopted at both parties' national conventions."

"Butchko said he favors immediate cessation of all bombing in North Vietnam as a step toward meaningful negotiations to end the war in Vietnam as soon as possible."

"Butchko is an attorney in Burbank."

In September Butchko went to Everett Burkhalter's home in North Hollywood, on a Saturday, and they discussed politics for over an hour.

In early September the Valley Green Sheet published a large article announcing that Butchko had been endorsed by the AFL-CIO. The Burbank Daily Review published a small article announcing this. Hubert Humphrey then said on the radio: "We have put it all together."

Butchko took his press release announcing his endorsement by the AFL-CIO into the offices of the Burbank Daily Review and handed to Ken Lubas, a Butchko supporter, who then showed it around and said this is news. The article in the Burbank Daily Review stated that John T. Butchko, the Democratic candidate for Congress in the Twenty-Seventh Congressional District, has been endorsed by the Los Angeles County Federation of Labor, Californians for Liberal Representation, and the International Association of Machinists.

In early September, Butchko had lunch with Arthur Carstens at a restaurant in downtown Burbank. Carstens then said that Butchko's name was still a political advantage for Butchko. In September the Record Ledger in Sunland-Tujunga, published Butchko's press release, stating that he had appointed Arthur Carstens to his campaign committee, and describing Arthur Carstens impressive background. This article stated: "Carstens has served as a senior Fulbright lecturer at the University of London and as a United States cultural affairs lecturer to Italy, Yugoslavia, Iran, Pakistan, Ceylon and India."

"He has also served as Chairman of the Los Angles City Labor-Management Committee, and is a senior staff member of the institute of industrial relations at UCLA."

In early September Butchko appeared at a dinner of labor union leaders in the East Valley, and he was introduced as the Democratic candidate for Congress in the Twenty-Seventh Congressional District.

Shortly after the Democratic National Convention, a reporter for Radio Station KBBQ in Burbank called Butchko on the telephone and asked for his opinion on the convention. Butchko said, among other things, that, "In contrast to the Republican convention, the Democratic Convention had an exchange of ideas."

In early September, Jim Quick, a Democrat in Lancaster, called Butchko and told him that Reinecke was going to speak at a local union meeting in Lancaster on a certain day and time. So Butchko went to Lancaster and he also spoke at this meeting. Butchko spoke in favor of civil rights for Blacks, and he told the people there that he had been endorsed by the AFL-CIO, which included their local union.

In September of 1968, Butchko received weekly publicity in the Daily Ledger Gazette in the Antelope Valley, including the publication of Butchko's press release stating that Reinecke had advocated escalation of the war in Vietnam and the mining of Haiphong Harbor, and that Butchko had called for immediate cessation of the bombing of North Vietnam as a first step toward negotiations to end the war in Vietnam.

In early September the Antelope Valley Press published Butchko's press release stating that Butchko would speak at a meeting of the Palmdale Democratic Club and describing Butchko's background and stating that Butchko favored raising the personal exemption for federal income taxes from 600 to at least 1,000 dollars. Butchko spoke at the September meeting of the Palmdale Democratic Club. He spoke on the issues and in favor of a complete bombing halt in North Vietnam. A speaker from a local chapter of the Americans for Democratic Action spoke and said that the ADA endorsed Humphrey, Cranston and Butchko. Mr. Chimbole, the mayor of Palmdale, was in attendance there. Members of the West Coast Longshoremen and Warehouse Workers Union told Butchko that they had put up his campaign signs in Boron. Mary Dermody, the local candidate for Assembly also spoke, and she also complimented Butchko on the quality of his speech.

In September, Butchko appeared at a meeting of the ILWU (International Longshore and Warehouse Workers Union) in San Pedro. At this meeting Butchko showed to a union member from Boron one of Butchko's press releases published in the Daily Ledger, Gazette (in the Antelope Valley) stating that Reinecke had called for escalation of the war in Vietnam and the mining of Haiphong Harbor. This union member said that this press published in the Daily Ledger Gazette was very damaging to Reinecke.

In early September there was a candidate day program at the Topanga Plaza Mall on a Saturday. Butchko and Reinecke both had booths there with their campaign sign, sheets on each of them. Butchko spoke with many people there and passed out his campaign card. Each candidate spoke there; Butchko said that he approved of the first act of de-escalation of the war in Vietnam, and that he hoped that there would be more de-escalation. Butchko spoke with Perry Pontac, who had been his friend at Glendale High School. Perry Pontac said that he would help Butchko. The Los Angeles Times, San Fernando Valley Section, showed a picture of Reinecke speaking there and also said that John T. Butchko, the Democratic candidate for Congress also spoke there.

In September the Valley Green Sheet published Butchko's press release stating that Butchko favored increasing social security retirement benefits and the details of Butchko's proposal.

In September the Valley Green Sheet published Butchko's press release stating that he would speak at a meeting of the Canoga Park Civic Association in Shadow Ranch

Park, and that Butchko had called for immediate cessation of the bombing of North Vietnam as a first step toward negotiations to end the war in Vietnam. Butchko spoke there in a theme of his full speech on Vietnam. Reinecke came there and spoke. Reinecke said that he (Reinecke) was a hawk and that he was campaigning desperately. After the speeches, a lady there said to Butchko, "Remember this is a Democratic area".

Throughout September and October, the San Fernando Valley Sun published a Butchko press release every week.

In September an Alan Cranston headquarters was opened in Encino.

In September an Alan Cranston headquarters was opened in the Fallbrook Mall in Canoga Park. The lady in charge of this headquarters was very friendly to Butchko, and she always had Butchko's campaign literature in the headquarters. In the latter part of September the Valley Green Sheet published Butchko's press release stating that he would speak at the grand opening of the headquarters and would speak on behalf of Alan Cranston and on behalf of his own campaign. In his speech at the grand opening, Butchko spoke about spreading peace throughout the world.

Butchko made frequent visits to the Cranston headquarters in Canoga Park, and in one of these visits he made a short speech to youngsters stuffing envelopes, in which speech Butchko urged them to work for Alan Cranston who stood for the principles of the peace movement.

In late September Butchko spoke at an outdoors party of the Sherman Oaks Democratic Club. There he talked with three girls from the Catholic Alumni Club, who told him that they had seen an article in a newspaper announcing that he would speak there. Butchko had joined the Catholic Alumni Club in 1964, and he always had many friends and acquaintances in that Club, and his name was listed in that Club's Directory of members.

Butchko had joined the Knights of Columbus in Burbank in early 1966. In the latter part of 1966 and early part of 1967, he was a member of the board of directors of the Cabrini Club, which managed the Knights of Columbus building in Burbank. Butchko attended most of the meetings of the Burbank Knights of Columbus in 1966 and 1967. In 1966, 1967 and 1968 Butchko had many friends and acquaintances in the Knights of Columbus in Burbank.

In September of 1968, Butchko appeared at the Knights of Columbus picnic on Scott Road in Burbank, where he spoke with many people and passed out his campaign cards.

One day in September when Butchko was at the office of the Valley Green Sheet, he saw that the Valley Green Sheet had in September republished in the central and eastern editions of the Valley Green Sheet, Butchko's press release attacking Reinecke's absentee voting record.

In late September of 1968, Butchko, with the help of Brian Kovsky, who worked for the Reminder, made and had printed a campaign brochure including two pictures of Butchko and a description of Butchko's background and Butchko's views including a statement that Butchko had consistently called for immediate cessation of the bombing of North Vietnam and negotiations with any and all parties to end the war in Vietnam as soon as possible. Butchko thereafter took this brochure with him and passed out the brochure to many people.

In late September or early October Butchko appeared at a large rally sponsored by Congressman George Brown at Hollywood High School. There Butchko was introduced to Eugene McCarthy, and they shook hands. Butchko sat between Richard Richards and Walter Karabian, a State Assemblyman who had been in the class ahead of Butchko at USC Law School. Butchko and Richards discussed Don White's campaign in the Twenty- Congressional District. And Richard Richards said to Butchko that he supposed that Butchko's running for Congress had qualified Butchko to be a trial lawyer. Butchko was introduced as the Democratic candidate for Congress in the Twenty-Seventh Congressional District. Walter Karabian spoke with Butchko and said that Butchko got good applause there when he was introduced. Richard Richards also said to Butchko, "You are making quite a splash." This was the first thing that Richard Richards said to Butchko there.

In September Butchko called Alice Sandoval who lived in Burbank in the Twenty-Seventh Congressional District, and they discussed Butchko's campaign. She said she would help Butchko. Alice Sandoval had been appointed to the Democratic State Central Committee by Jack Howard in 1966. In about September of 1968 Culver Van Buren again told Butchko that he would help with Butchko's campaign.

Throughout 1968, Butchko appeared at many headquarters' meetings and made many visits to the various headquarters where he spoke with the people there.

In September Butchko spoke to the entire student body of Chaminade Catholic Preparatory School in the West Valley, Butchko there gave his full speech on the war in Vietnam. After Butchko's speech, the entire student body stood up and applauded Butchko.

In about September of 1968, when Butchko visited the offices of the Newhall Signal, he saw a lady employee with a Butchko bumper sticker on the wall above her desk.

In the first half of September, Butchko was visited at his office by a man he had befriended at the Antelope Valley Fair. Butchko recorded a speech to be taken to and delivered at a meeting of the Rosamond Democratic Club. This friend took Butchko's recorded speech and had it played at a meeting of the Rosamond Democratic Club. He told Butchko that a newspaper in Rosamond published an article stating that Butchko would speak at a meeting of the Rosamond Democratic Club.

Every week in September and October, The Reminder published a press release from Butchko. The Reminder was circulated in Woodland Hills.

In September, Mary Dermody's campaign workers displayed Butchko's campaign signs at the Vallermo Festival in the Antelope Valley.

In September, at a meeting of the Fifty-Seventh Assembly District Democratic Council, the members discussed whether the council should have a headquarters. Some opposed having a headquarters because they were not yet supporting Humphrey. Leonard Maizlich said he was opposed to having a headquarters if the campaign workers did not carry Humphrey's campaign literature. Butchko said he favored headquarters where workers could carry Humphrey's literature if they wanted but did not have to if they did not want to.

In late September, Butchko appeared at the grand opening of the Burbank Democratic headquarters in the Golden Mall in downtown Burbank. Eugene Radding presided over this grand opening. Leonard Maizlich, the Democratic candidate for

Assembly in the Fifty-Seventh Assembly District was there and he saw Butchko, and he talked briefly with Butchko. Mary Dermody, the Democratic candidate for Assembly in the Sixth-Second Assembly District, was there and she saw Butchko. Her husband, John Dermody, was there and Butchko spoke with him. Jack Howard was there and he saw Butchko. At this headquarters opening Butchko exchanged greetings with the lady who had been in charge of the McCarthy headquarters in Burbank before the primary. The headquarters had campaign signs for Alan Cranston, John T. Butchko and Don White on the door. The ladies operating this headquarters were friendly to Butchko, and campaign workers carried Butchko's campaign cards to residences in the Twenty-Seventh Congressional District part of Burbank until the general election.

On one occasion Butchko visited this headquarters and spoke with a student on his way home from Bellarmine-Jefferson High School, and after this one of the ladies managing the headquarters said that Butchko had made that student's day.

In late September or early October, after the grand opening of the Democratic headquarters in Burbank, Butchko appeared and spoke at a large rally for Alan Cranston at a hall in Saugus. Butchko was introduced by Alan Cranston's wife. Butchko had been told about this rally by some official Cranston workers at the grand opening of the Democratic Headquarters in Burbank. At this rally, in his speech, Butchko attacked Reinecke as a hawk, and attacked Reinecke for Reinecke's voting against the Fair Housing Act of 1968. Butchko also spoke with John Newhall, the editor of the Newhall Signal, and with Lionel Rolfe, a reporter with the Newhall Signal.

In September or October of 1968, at one of Butchko's speeches on the war in Vietnam at a candidate's forum in the West Valley, Pat McGhee, the local Republican

Assemblyman said that he did not like to have his country called an aggressor. Butchko never used the word "aggressor". He just stated the facts and the history of the war in Vietnam.

In late September or early October, Butchko visited the Democratic Headquarters in Lancaster, and spoke with people there, and he put a large stack of his brochures in there. This headquarters was managed by Mary Dermody, the local Democratic candidate for Assembly, who was actively supporting Butchko.

In early October Butchko appeared at a Democratic candidate's day program at the Marquardt aerospace plant in Van Nuys. Butchko sat on a platform with James Corman, and Butchko was introduced as the Democratic candidate for Congress in the Twenty-Seventh District. Senator Hughes of Iowa spoke there. Butchko spoke with many workers there and passed out his brochure to many workers there. After this, Butchko had dinner with two executives of that plant and they discussed politics.

In about October of 1968, Butchko spoke at a candidates form at San Fernando Valley State College in Northridge. Butchko spoke mostly on the war in Vietnam, and his views on that war.

Toward the end of September, Butchko and Brian made an individual campaign brochure, which Butchko would use effectively. This brochure put Butchko's picture on the front and stated: "Its time for a change" at the top, and above Butchko's picture it said John T. Butchko for Congress, and next to Butchko's picture, it said, "he can do more for you."

This brochure stated: "John Butchko has consistently called for immediate cessation of the bombing of North Vietnam and negotiations with any and all parties to end the war in Vietnam as soon as possible."

"John Butchko favors legislation to protect collective bargaining rights for working men and women. He favors maintenance of a vital aerospace industry in our district. He favors lower interest rates and other programs directed toward a renewal of business growth in our district."

"John Butchko favors increasing the personal exemption for federal income taxes from $600.00 to at least $1,000.00. He favors elimination of the 10% surcharge on income taxes and the elimination of taxes on foreign travel."

"John Butchko favors preservation of our redwood forests, our national parks and our wilderness areas. He favors preservation of the family farm. He would introduce legislation establishing low-cost vacation village parks in our remote countryside areas to provide recreational, educational and cultural facilities for vacations."

"John Butchko favors more adequate income security for a senior citizen."

"John Butchko believes that jobs must be created for all who are able to work. He believes that the private sector should provide most of them with the public sector, becoming the employer of last resort, where necessary. Job training for the hard-core unemployed should be pursued by private industry with the help of government."

"John Butchko favors implementation of the Report of the National Advisory Commission on civil disorders."

"John Butchko has spent much time meeting with the people of the Twenty-Seventh Congressional District and discussing their problems. They know that he can do more for them. John Butchko is a Democrat who welcomes the support of Republicans and others who agree that our new Twenty-Seventh Congressional District needs better representation in Congress."

Butchko's entire background appeared on the last page, including the statement that he was a member of the Order of the Coif, an honorary legal fraternity.

In October Butchko debated with Reinecke at Chatsworth High School before the entire student body in the auditorium there. After the debate, some students there told Butchko that he had won that debate. In speaking there, Butchko said that he favored immediate cessation of the bombing of North Vietnam.

In October of 1968, the Valley Green Sheet published Butchko's press release stating that Butchko would speak at a candidate's forum of the Van Nuys Airport Chamber of Commerce at the Skytrails Restaurant in Van Nuys. Before the speeches, the man in charge of this candidate's forum told Butchko that Reinecke had been there and left there without speaking. Butchko gave a speech in the theme of his full speech on Vietnam at this candidate's forum.

In October, a Mr. MacDonald, who had been Butchko's American History teacher at Glendale High School came into the Democratic headquarters on the Golden Mall in Burbank. Butchko was there. Mr. MacDonald said in the hearing of the headquarters managers: Butchko was a liberal even in high school. "That's a good sign."

In October, Butchko spoke at the cafeteria of the Hughes Aerospace plant in Canoga Park. Butchko gave a speech in the theme of his full speech on the war in Vietnam. After the speech Butchko was greeted outside by a distinguished looking gentleman and by two girls with straw hats and Butchko bumper stickers around their hats. This man said to Butchko: " You are like Reinecke, young and personable."

On October 1, Butchko's billboards went up. There was one on Sherman Way in Canoga Park, one on Devonshire Boulevard in Chatsworth, one on Ventura Boulevard in Sherman Oaks, and three in Burbank, including one on Olive Avenue directly across the street from Saint Finnbars Church, where everyone who went to that church had to see it. There where two in Palmdale, two in Lancaster and one in Mojave.

In October Butchko spoke with Travers Devine on the telephone and Travers said that he heard that Butchko's billboards were in good locations.

In about October, Butchko spoke at a candidate's forum of the Chatsworth Business and Professional Women's Club at a restaurant in Chatsworth. Reinecke also spoke there. Butchko gave a speech in the theme of his full speech on Vietnam. After this event, Butchko attended a meeting at the headquarters of the Sixty-Fourth Assembly District Democratic Council, where Guy Raner, the local Democratic candidate for Assembly, said that Butchko had spoken like McCarthy at that candidate's forum.

In about October, Butchko spoke at a candidate's forum sponsored by the League of Women Voters at a large auditorium in Ridgecrest. Before the speeches, Butchko had dinner with some persons associated with the forum, and one of them, a lady said: "It's good to see these beautiful Democratic candidates." Butchko gave a speech in the theme of his full speech on Vietnam. The auditorium was crowded. After his speech Butchko exchanged greetings with an attorney, who had been in Butchko's class in law school, and who had spoken on behalf of Alan Cranston at this candidate's forum. Butchko gave a large stack of his brochures to a local Democrat who said he

97

would distribute them in the area. Right after Butchko's speech, a Republican Assemblyman, Mr. Stacey said to Butchko, "We will see you again."

In October the editor of the Newhall Signal, John Newhall along with Lionel Rolfe, a Signal reporter took Butchko to dinner at a restaurant in Newhall. Butchko told him that Butchko was supporting Humphrey.

On about October 10, the Valley Green Sheet published an article stating: "John T. Butchko, the Democratic candidate in the Twenty-Seventh Congressional District today had charged that the incumbent Ed Reinecke is claiming the introduction of various bills at a time when it is too late for Congress to pass them in this election year."

Butchko said,"Reinecke's public relations efforts are based on his desire to avoid the real issues, such as his hawkish views on Vietnam and his opposition to necessary domestic reforms."

The Reminder published a similar article on October 10. This was helpful publicity for Butchko in the Valley Green Sheet.

In October Butchko spoke with the new editor of the Tolucan at the offices of that newspaper. That editor there gave Butchko a campaign contribution.

In October Butchko received a letter from Travers Devine, in which Travers said that "he prayed for a Butchko victory."

In October, Butchko spoke at a meeting of the Porter Ranch Homeowners Association. Butchko there gave a speech in the theme of his full speech on Vietnam.

In October, Butchko spoke at a candidate's forum of the United Methodist Church in Woodland Hills. Butchko there gave a speech in the theme of his full speech on Vietnam.

In early October Butchko attended Muskie's arrival at the Burbank airport, and gave to Muskie's wife his individual campaign brochure, and he exchanged greetings with Muskie. Shortly there after Muskie said that if he favored a bombing halt in North Vietnam he would not say this in a press release, or such, but would write a letter to Lyndon Johnson.

In the first half of October, Hubert Humphrey made a major televised speech on Vietnam. First he defended the support, which he had always given to the Vietnam War policies of Lyndon Johnson. Then he said that if elected he would stop the bombing of all of North Vietnam and negotiate, but if the North Vietnamese did not show good faith, he would reserve the right to resume the bombing.

In October Butchko spoke at a candidate's forum of the Glass Bottle Blowers Association in the Newhall-Saugus area. There Butchko gave a speech in the theme of his full speech on Vietnam. Butchko gave a stack of his brochures to a Democrat there, who said that he would distribute them locally. Reinecke's field representative also spoke there; and when Lionel Rolfe asked him a question, he said: "You are from the Newhall Signal." And he refused to answer Lionel Rolfe's question. John Newhall, the editor of the Newhall Signal was also there.

In October of 1968, the Los Angeles Times (all editions) published a candidate's section describing Butchko's and Reinecke's backgrounds and views. This candidate's section included a statement that Butchko favors immediate cessation of the bombing of North Vietnam.

In October the Valley Green Sheet published Butchko's press release describing in detail Butchko's plans for ensuring clean water and for eliminating water pollution.

In 1967 and 1968, Butchko's speeches on the war in Vietnam had the effect of moving the country.

In every week in September and October, The Reminder published at least one of Butchko's press releases.

In the latter part of October the Newhall Signal published an article stating "Congressman Edwin Reinecke was called to task yesterday by his Democratic challenger, John Butchko for sending out 'campaign literature' at the taxpayer's expense."

"But Butchko qualified his criticism of Valencia Valley's incumbent Republican representative by adding that he felt this showed that Reinecke was getting 'desperate'".

"Reinecke is putting on a big campaign. He must be worried", Butchko said.

"Butchko directed his criticism at the Congressman's "Reports from Washington" mailed last week to every home in Valencia Valley."

"The literature identifies itself as not being printed at government expense, but the cost of mailing it, usually the biggest expense of a local campaign, came out of the Congressman's "franking privilege", Butchko said."

"Most incumbents do not use their franking privilege so close to the election because most realize that this constitutes a serious abuse of the privilege, Butchko said."

"Butchko pointed out that irony of the whole episode was that while Reinecke was mailing literature to the voters at taxpayer expense, the literature itself has purported to call for economy in government."

"This, Butchko believes shows that Reinecke has become both erratic and desperate in the last few weeks before the election".

In October the Butchko Raner Committee prepared and had printed with the help of Brian Kovsky, a big brochure supporting Alan Cranston, John Butchko and Guy Raner, the Democratic candidate in the Sixty-Fourth Assembly District. This brochure described the backgrounds of Butchko and Raner and the views of each of these three candidates. This brochure had pictures of all three candidates, including three pictures of Butchko. The listing of Butchko's views included the statement that Butchko had consistently called for immediate cessation of the bombing of North Vietnam and negotiations with any and all parties to end the war in Vietnam as soon as possible. This brochure included a statement that Butchko had been endorsed by the AFL-CIO and the United Workers and numerous other organizations. This brochure included a long list of members of the Butchko Raner Committee. Underneath Alan Cranston's picture it said, "PEACE". Underneath Butchko's picture it said "COURAGE". Under Guy Raner's picture it said, "HONESTY". This brochure announced support for Stanley Scheinbaum in the Thirteenth Congressional District, John Pratt in the Twenty-Eighth Congressional District, Gerald (Jerry) Porter in the Twenty-Third State Senate District, and Leonard Maizlich in the Fifty-Seventh Assembly District. It was a very large and very attractive brochure. There was a tremendous amount of these brochures in the headquarters of the Sixty-Fourth Assembly District Democratic Council on Sherman Way in Canoga Park.

In the start of October through the general election day, there was a Humphrey headquarters in Northridge. This headquarters was managed by Fred Ball, who told Butchko that campaign workers were carrying Butchko's campaign cards from this headquarters to residences in the Twenty-Seventh Congressional District. In this headquarters there was a tremendous amount of Butchko's campaign cards.

The headquarters of the Sixty-Fourth Assembly District Democratic Council on Sherman Way in Canoga Park opened shortly after the endorsing convention of the Twenty-Seventh Congressional District Democratic Council, and it remained open until the general election on November 6th. Ted Lane was in charge of and managed this headquarters. There was always Butchko's campaign literature in this headquarters.

In October campaign workers started carrying and distributing the brochure of the Butchko Raner Committee to residences from the headquarters of the Sixty-Fourth Assembly District Democratic Council and from Alan Cranston's headquarters on the Fallbrook Mall in Canoga Park.

Brian Kovsky told Butchko the workers at Alan Cranston's headquarters in Encino also carried the brochure of the Butchko Raner Committee to residences.

In October, Butchko debated Reinecke at the meeting of the Burbank Chamber of Commerce. They debated the situation and war in Vietnam. A reporter from the Burbank Daily Review was present.

In the latter part of October the Los Angeles Times, all sections, published a candidates description describing Butchko and Reinecke's backgrounds and views and stating that Butchko favored immediate cessation of the bombing of North Vietnam. In this and most candidates' descriptions, Reinecke said he favored an honorable peace. By this he meant a military victory.

In October Butchko spoke at a candidate's forum at the Valley Beth Shalom Temple in Encino. There he gave a speech in the theme of his full speech on Vietnam. Butchko placed a stack of the brochure of the Butchko-Raner Committee on the table for candidate's literature. Reinecke also spoke there and said that he (Reinecke) was campaigning desperately.

In October, Butchko was invited by Escoe Fuller to speak at a meeting of the Burbank Board of Realtors, but Butchko had a prior engagement.

In October, the Butchko-Raner Committee put on a rally for Butchko on a Sunday in the football field and grandstand of Taft High School in Woodland Hills. Butchko gave a strong speech attacking Reinecke as a hawk. Stanley Scheinbaum also spoke, and gave a speech on the situation in Vietnam. Tom Bradley also spoke there. A representative for John Pratt was there, and he exchanged greetings with Butchko. The brochure of the Butchko-Raner Committee was passed out at this rally. An article in the Reminder announced that this rally would take place and Radio Station KGIL announced that this rally would take place. Jeanne Caya attended this rally and she told Butchko that he sounded good.

In October Butchko visited the political editor of the Daily Ledger Gazette at the offices of that paper in Lancaster. That editor said that unfortunately it looked like the L.A. Times would endorse Reinecke. The way he said this indicated that he wanted Butchko to win.

In the latter part of October, Butchko appeared and spoke at a party for Democratic Party campaign workers at the Machinists Union Hall in Burbank. Butchko pointed out and criticized Reinecke's anti-labor voting record and Butchko passed out to the people there the brochure of the Butchko-Raner Committee.

In late October the Los Angeles Times, San Fernando Valley Section, published a candidates description entitled: "GOP Incumbent Reinecke Facing Challenge of Democrat Butchko." This article stated: "John T. Butchko", a resident of 123 N. Myers St., Burbank, Butchko, 31, is an attorney and graduate of the USC School of Law, where he also received a Masters degree.

"He is a member of Phi Beta Kappa and the Order of the Coif, an honorary legal fraternity and served as an associate editor of the Southern California Law Review."

"He was a member of the Los Angeles County Democratic Central Committee from 1966 to June, 1968 and has the endorsement of the California Machinists non-Partisan Political League, the California Democratic Council, and Californians for Liberal Representation."

"He favors a return of federal taxes to the states for education and to relieve the property taxpayer. He urges removal of financial barriers to higher education, and increased federal assistance to cities and states for pollution control."

"He said that to protect the value of the dollar, renewed business growth in a peacetime economy should be sought, and the personal exemption for federal income taxes should be increased from $600 to $1,000. He seeks elimination of the 10% surcharge on income taxes."

"Butchko has called for immediate cessation of the bombing of North Vietnam and negotiations with all parties to end the war."

This candidate's description included pictures of Butchko and Reinecke. In most of the candidates descriptions Reinecke said he favored an honorable peace. By this he meant a military victory.

In October, the Burbank Daily Review published a similar candidate's description of Butchko and Reinecke, including a picture of each candidate, and a statement that Butchko favors immediate cessation of the bombing of Vietnam and negotiations with any and all parties to end the war as soon as possible. This candidate's section in the Burbank Daily Review stated, inter alia, that "Butchko is a member of the Democratic State Central Committee and that he has been a member of the County Central Committee. He has been endorsed by the political committees of the AFL-CIO, the United Auto Workers (UAW), and the International Association of Machinists (IAM).

In 1968, Butchko sent out a tremendous number of press releases.

On October 24, the Greek Catholic Union Messenger mailed throughout the United States published an article stating that, "Mrs. Anna Butchko, formerly of Erie, Pa., and now residing in California and who is a member of the Greek Catholic Union, has informed us that her grandson, Attorney John T. Butchko, is the Democratic Candidate for Congress in the Twenty-Seventh Congressional District of California. He lives in Burbank, California and attends St. Mary's Byzantine Catholic Church in Van Nuys. He is of Carpatho Russian (Russian) extraction and formerly of Cleveland, Ohio.

"Attorney Butchko is a graduate of the University of Southern California School of Law and has served as a research attorney for the United States District Court for the Southern District of California."

"Sincerest best wishes as are extended to candidate Butchko in his quest for a seat in the House of Representatives in Washington, D.C."

With Brian Kovsky's help, Butchko made and had published his full advertisement in the Valley Green Sheet on Thursday, October 31 and Friday, November 1; and in the Reminder on Thursday, October 31 and on Thursday October 24, and in the Canyon Crier on November 1, 1968.

Butchko's advertisement had Butchko's picture, and a statement that Butchko was an attorney, and was endorsed by the AFL-CIO, the United Auto Workers and numerous other organizations. This full advertisement includes a full statement of Butchko's views, including a statement that "John T. Butchko has consistently called for immediate cessation of the bombing of North Vietnam as a step toward meaningful negotiations to end the war."

This advertisement also stated: "John T. Butchko favors legislation to protect collective bargaining rights for working men and women. He favors maintenance of a vital aerospace industry within the district. He favors lower interest rates and other programs directed toward a renewal of business growth."

"John T. Butchko favors increasing the personal exemption for federal income taxes from $600 to at least $1,000. He favors elimination of the 10% surcharge on income taxes and elimination of taxes on foreign travel."

"He favors a return of federal taxes to the states for education and to relieve the property taxpayer. He favors removal of all financial barriers to higher education. He favors lowering the voting age to eighteen."

"John T. Butchko favors presentation of our redwood forests, our national parks and our wilderness areas. He favors establishment of low cost vacation village parks in remote country areas to provide recreational educational and cultural facilities for vacationers."

"John T. Butchko favors more adequate income security for our senior citizens. He believes that jobs should be provided for all who are able to work. Job training for the hard core unemployed should be pursued by private industry with the help of government."

"John T. Butchko favors establishment of a nationwide primary."

This advertisement said that Reinecke has continually advocated deeper military involvement in Vietnam. This advertisement also described Reinecke's absentee voting record; that Reinecke was absent on 53 of the yea-nay roll call votes in the 1966 session. This advertisement said that Reinecke had voted for the 10% surcharge on income taxes; and that Reinecke had voted for cuts in expenditures resulting in loss of aerospace contracts in the San Fernando Valley.

In 1968 Butchko's name combined with his being unopposed in the primary and his aggressive campaign (including his speeches on the war in Vietnam) made Butchko the most effective peace candidate for any office.

Butchko placed an advertisement in the Tolucan on October 31; the Tolucan was delivered to every residence in Toluca Lake and a large part of Burbank, and in a part of

North Hollywood. This advertisement described Butchko's background and stated that Butchko favored immediate cessation of the bombing of North Vietnam as a step toward meaningful negotiations to end the war.

In October Butchko arranged to have all these advertisements published. Butchko's arranging for these advertisements put a tremendous amount of pressure on Johnson.

On October 31, the Record Ledger, circulated in Sunland-Tujunga published an advertisement placed by the Sunland-Tujunga Democratic Club stating that the Sunland-Tujunga Democratic Club endorsed Alan Cranston for Senate; John T. Butchko for Congress in the Twenty-Seventh District; and that these candidates could be counted on to work for peace.

In October, the publication of State of California Chamber of Commerce was published, containing descriptions of Congressional candidates. This issue had Butchko's picture and a statement that Butchko had called for de-escalation of the war in Vietnam and negotiations to end the war.

Shortly before the general election the California Farm Bureau Federation published an issue describing Congressional candidates. This issue included a picture of John T. Butchko and a statement that he favored extending the protection of the national labor laws to farm workers, and some details.

Late in October, there was a large candidate's forum for all the candidates on the ballot in any part of Kern County. Butchko secured the services of a member of the Sherman Oaks Democratic Club to represent Butchko's at this candidate's forum.

Afterwards Butchko's representative told Butchko that his speech and answers to questions went well.

On October 31 of 1968, Lyndon Johnson announced that he was stopping the bombing in the Southern portion of North Vietnam. Then negotiations were immediately commenced between the United States and North Vietnam. Butchko's aggressive campaign was the major factor in the movement that induced Johnson to make this bombing halt. There would have been no bombing halt in 1968 without the effect of Butchko's campaign. After the bombing halt, Lionel Rolfe a reporter for the Newhall Signal called Butchko and told him not to give up.

On Friday November 1, the Valley Green Sheet, the Los Angeles Herald Examiner and the Daily Ledger Gazette in the Antelope Valley published candidate's sections. The candidate's section in the Valley Green Sheet described Butchko's background and his views, including a statement that throughout his campaign Butchko had consistently called for immediate cessation of the bombing of North Vietnam as a first step toward negotiations to end the war. In most of the candidate's sections, Reinecke said he favored an honorable peace. By this he meant a military victory. The candidate's section in the Daily Ledger Gazette had an extremely long description of Butchko's and Reinecke's views. The candidate's section in the Herald Examiner described Butchko's background and his views; including a statement that Butchko had called for immediate cessation of the bombing of North Vietnam and negotiations with all parties to end the war.

The candidate's page in the Daily Ledger Gazette also stated that Butchko had called for immediate cessation of the bombing of North Vietnam, and negotiations with all parties to end the war.

The candidate's sections in the Valley Green Sheet and the Daily Ledger Gazette also included pictures of Butchko and Reinecke.

The candidate's section in the Valley Green Sheet was entitled: "Reinecke Facing Challenge by John Butchko in Twenty-Seventh Congressional Race".

On November 1, the Burbank Daily Review and the Glendale News Press published an article reporting on the Butchko-Reinecke debate. This article stated: "How to end the Vietnam War emerged as the central issue in a candidates forum before the Chamber of Commerce on Monday."

"Opposite views on the subject were expressed by Republican incumbent Ed Reinecke and John Butchko Democratic challenger for the Twenty-Seventh District seat in the House of Representatives."

"I (Reinecke) am convinced from my knowledge of how the Communists operate, that the only way to deal with them is of a position of strength."

"The Congressman advocated cutting off enemy supply lines, closing harbors and bombing all necessary targets to rush the war to an end."

"Of course, I hope the peace talks in Paris are successful, but the Communists will negotiate only if we are tough."

"I talked with a man recently who had been in Vietnam 15 years and he predicted that the war will drag on another 15-20 years if we don't stop dilly-dallying around."

"Reinecke called for new Republican leadership in the White House and Congress to end the war."

"Butchko said he, too, sought to end the war. However, short of the use of nuclear weapons, there can be no military victory in Vietnam."

"Butchko said the United States became involved in the Vietnam conflict on a great scale in 1965, entering what was essentially a civil war."

"He called for a complete halt to bombing of North Vietnam and negotiations to end the war."

"Bombing of North Vietnam has not stopped troop movement," he said.

"The Vietnam Communist leaders have indicated clearly that they will not truly negotiate with the bombing going on."

"The Vietnam war has divided our people, depressed our economy and depressed the nation's young people."

"There is no simple formula to negotiations, they would be difficult. There really is no satisfactory conclusion to such a war."

"I propose a multilateral agreement among many nations ensuring the right of the Vietnamese people to choose their own destiny."

On November 1, there was received in the mail by well over 15,000 residences the American Aeronaut, the newspaper of the Lockheed Machinists Union. This issue endorsed Butchko, published Butchko's picture, said that Butchko is a Democrat, and stated that Butchko favors increasing the personal exemption for federal income taxes from $600 to $1,000.

On November 1, the Newhall Signal editorial criticized Nixon and Humphrey, and endorsed Alan Cranston for Senate, and Butchko for Congress.

On November 1, the San Fernando Valley Sun published an article stating that State Senator Tom Carrell endorsed certain candidates. These candidates included John Butchko in the Twenty-Seventh Congressional District. Very shortly before the general election, Lionel Rolfe, a reporter for the Newhall Signal called Butchko and said that he heard that Tom Carrell endorsed Butchko.

Shortly before the general election, brochures of the Los Angeles County Federation of Labor, AFL-CIO, were circulated where the members of the workers' union in the Federation worked, including Universal Studios, where Butchko's father worked. This brochure endorsed Humphrey, Muskie, Alan Cranston and Congressional candidates by district, including John T. Butchko, in the Twenty-Seventh Congressional District.

In October of 1968, a Mr. Gelson, an owner of Gelson's Supermarkets, told Brian Kovsky that of all the Democratic candidates running against Republican incumbents, Butchko had the best chance to win.

The Valley Green Sheet published a description of Butchko's background and Reinecke's background in the article announcing their debate before the Burbank Chamber of Commerce.

The Valley Green Sheet published Butchko's attack on Reinecke's absentee voting record in 1966 an extra time in September in the Eastern and Central editions.

The Valley Green Sheet published four articles on Butchko in 1967. The Valley Green Sheet published 44 articles on Butchko in 1968.

The editor of the Reminder, who was also the owner, printed special editions of that newspaper to record Butchko's press releases for posterity. These special editions showed that Butchko sent out a tremendous number of press releases in 1968. These special editions were separate from the editions that were circulated. These special editions were not circulated.

In 1968, Butchko sent out a tremendous number of press releases.

The Burbank Daily Review published two articles on Butchko in 1967.

The Burbank Daily Review published nine articles on Butchko in 1968.

In 1968, newspapers published over 120 articles on Butchko. All of this publicity for Butchko had a tremendous effect on advancing the peace movement.

Butchko's sending out his press releases to many newspapers, radio stations and other media had a tremendous effect on advancing the peace movement.

On the Saturday before the general election, Butchko supporters put Butchko's individual campaign brochure on all the cars in the Fallbrook mall's parking lot in Canoga Park.

On the Sunday evening before the general election, Butchko spoke at a Democratic rally in a large hall in the Sportsman Lodge. Jim Corman and David Negri spoke there. This large hall was crowded with campaign workers. Butchko said, to vote against Nixon again, and that "We cannot afford to have Nixon as President," and "get the Democrats out to vote," and that "The Democratic Party is the only party capable of producing national leadership." This speech by Butchko gave a big boost to Humphrey.

Butchko's bringing about both bombing halts in 1968, made the 1968 presidential election closer than it otherwise would have been, and enabled Humphrey to come closer than he otherwise would have come.

In 1968, Butchko sent all of his press releases to the newspaper in Ridgecrest, to the Mojave Desert News, to the newspaper in Tehachapi, to the newspaper in Lebec, to the Daily Ledger Gazette, to the Antelope Valley Press, to the Newhall Signal, to the Newhall Saugus Sun and Sylmar Breeze, to the Record Ledger, to the Glendale Independent, to the Valley Green Sheet, to the San Fernando Valley Section of the Los Angeles Times, to the Burbank Daily Review, to the Burbank Independent, to the San Fernando Valley Times, to the Sherman Oaks Sun, to the Reminder, the Northridger, to the Canoga Park Chronicle, to Radio Station KBBQ in Burbank, to the American Aeronaut in Burbank and to the City News Service. Starting sometime in February, Butchko sent all his press releases to the San Fernando Valley State College Sundial. From January or February of 1968, Butchko sent all of his press releases to the Montrose Ledger, also called the Ledger, until May of 1968.

After the primary, Butchko sent all of his press releases to NBC in Burbank, to Radio Station KGIL in San Fernando, to another newspaper in the Newhall-Saugus area, to the Bakersfield Californian, to KERO TV in Bakersfield, to Radio Station KLOA in Ridgecrest, and to the San Fernando Valley Sun.

Starting sometime during the general election campaign, Butchko sent all of his press releases to the Glendale News Press, to La Opinion, to Radio Station KIEV, to three Senior Citizen Periodicals, one of which endorsed all the Democratic candidates for Congress, to the Canyon Crier, and to the Tolucan. The Canyon Crier was sent to every

114

residence in the Hollywood Hills. The Tolucan was delivered to every residence in Toluca Lake and a large part of western Burbank and to part of North Hollywood.

In October, the new editor of the Tolucan gave Butchko a campaign contribution in the offices of the Tolucan. In October the Tolucan published at least one of its own articles favorable to Butchko.

Starting sometime in February through the primary, Butchko sent all his press releases to the Hollywood Citizen News, which went out of business shortly after the primary. The Newhall Saugus Sun and Sylmar Breeze also went out of business shortly after the primary.

Voter registration in the Twenty-Seventh Congressional District at the time of the November 5 general election was almost evenly divided between the two major parties. The Democratic registration was 130,937; the Republican registration was 123,002. There were over 3,000 registered voters of the American Independent Party. There were approximately 1,000 Peace and Freedom registrants. Butchko received 62,824 votes. Reinecke received 162,854 votes. Butchko's percentages were lowest in the Sixty-Second Assembly District where Masons were most numerous. In the primary, he had done at least as well in the Sixty-Second Assembly District as elsewhere considering that was the part of the new Congressional District which had also been in the old Congressional District and the part where Reinecke was best known. In 1968 there was a significant backlash vote because of the urban riots in 1967 and 1968.

Butchko campaign expenditures between the primary and general election were only $3,100.

After the election the Valley Green Sheet published an article stating that Reinecke had defeated Butchko in a heavily Democratic District which had been gerrymandered for Butchko's benefit. Actually the district had been gerrymandered to protect Reinecke, and a 51% Democratic district had never been regarded as a heavily Democratic district in California.

All the Democratic candidates running for Congress against incumbent Republicans in Los Angeles County were defeated by large margins. Butchko's percentage of the total vote adjusted to party registration was higher than that received by the Democratic candidate for Congress in the Thirty-Second Congressional District in Los Angeles County. An incumbent, Assemblyman named David Negri lost his seat in the San Fernando Valley's Forty-First Assembly District although Democrats were sixty percent of the two party registrations there.

All of the incumbent Congressmen in California were re-elected in 1968 because of the gerrymander.

Butchko's name combined with his being unopposed in the primary made Butchko the most effective peace candidate for any office in 1968.

Right after the general election, Butchko received a telegram from Humphrey stating "You have my sincere regrets on your election loss. I hope that you will continue in the search for a better America and a more peaceful world for which you gave so much of yourself during your campaign."

After the general election of 1968, Butchko was under video surveillance by more people than anyone else. This made Butchko tremendously effective in advancing the peace movement, and made Butchko the most effective person on advancing the

116

peace movement. After 1968 Butchko made all the difference on ending the war in Vietnam.

Shortly after the general election of 1968 Butchko met with Tom Carrell at Tom Carrell's office in San Fernando. State Senator Tom Carrell said that Butchko had not done badly in the general election of 1968, and said to "play it by ear"; and "maybe next year."

In November after the election, the legal secretaries of Glendale and Burbank sponsored a large banquet for attorneys and secretaries in Glendale and Burbank. Culver VanBuren spoke at this banquet. Butchko was there, and he was introduced specially as a friend by Jerry Coons' legal secretary. Jerry Coons was an attorney in Los Angeles. This banquet was held at a large hall in Burbank.

At this event, the husband of Liz Atkerson said to Butchko that, in the general election, he voted for Butchko, but not for Humphrey.

It was unprecedented that a Slav, such as John Butchko, was a Democratic nominee for Congress in the San Fernando Valley.

Being unopposed in the primary combined with his name made Butchko the most effective peace candidate.

In 1968, Butchko was the only peace candidate, who was unopposed in the primary, except perhaps for some incumbents.

Butchko made all the difference in de-escalating and ending the war in Vietnam.

In November of 1968, in an elevator at Universal Studios, Butchko met a man who had seen Butchko speak at a meeting of the Porter Ranch Homeowners Association

117

in October. This man told Butchko that getting elected to Congress was a tough nut to crack, but that he thought that Butchko did good. Butchko was the major factor in bringing about all of the bombing halts and all of the troop withdrawls.

In November or December of 1968, Butchko received a letter from the Chairman of the Democratic State Central Committee stating that Butchko was entitled to appoint one Associate Member of the Democratic State Central Committee. Butchko appointed a liberal Democrat who was a member of the Knights of Columbus in Burbank.

In January of 1969, Governor Reagan appointed Reinecke Lieutenant Governor of California to fill a vacancy. Reagan's appointment of Reinecke gave a big boost to Butchko and thereby to the cause of peace.

When Reinecke was appointed Lieutenant Governor, an article in the Los Angeles Herald Examiner said that Butchko could run for Reinecke's vacant seat in Congress.

In January of 1969, Butchko attended a party at Helen Greenberg's house in Van Nuys. Doctor Doctor, a candidate for the Los Angeles School Board, spoke and said: "Isn't it nice to have John Butchko here today."

The main reason why Nixon did not resume the bombing of North Vietnam for such a long time (over three years) was Butchko's political potential.

Late in December of 1968, Butchko had landed a job in a prestigious law firm in the One Wilshire Building in downtown Los Angeles. The name of the firm was Dryden, Harrington and Swartz. When Butchko was hired he was told that he could not run for office for five years. Butchko had moved his office furniture into his large apartment in

118

Burbank, and he was ready to leave the firm and open his own office in a very short period of time. Butchko attended the Christmas party of this law firm before December 25, 1968, and all the buzz at this party was about Butchko's having run for Congress. Butchko could even practice law in his own large apartment. Butchko's apartment was the only apartment on the lot.

After Nixon was elected President, Butchko was under more video surveillance by more people than anyone else. This made Butchko tremendously effective in advancing the peace movement, and made Butchko the most effective person in advancing the peace movement.

In January of 1969, just outside the County Law Library, Butchko met Betty Tom, who had been in Butchko's class in the USC Law School and also had graduated from the law school; and Betty Tom said that she thought that Butchko had done good in his election contest.

In December of 1968, Butchko attended a gathering of Democrats in Anaheim. There Butchko spoke very briefly with Everett Burkhalter.

Shortly after Reinecke's appointment in January, Butchko attended an open meeting and party sponsored by Democratic Party groups in Los Angeles. Butchko spoke with people there. Muskie spoke before the large turnout, and said that he had lost his first election campaign for public office, and that he thought the best part of running was the opportunity to change people's minds. Sigmund Arywitz, who was still Chairman of the Los Angeles County Federation of Labor, and who it seemed had damaged Butchko's campaign before the primary, said that the Democrats had lost the Presidential election because "we (the Democrats) did not all worship in the same

119

church." This was the first time Butchko had heard anyone publicly express a religious interpretation of the 1968 elections. Arywitz then went on to say that there was a "kind of candidates that we (apparently meaning the Democratic Party) have to kill." Butchko thought that Arywitz's brief description of this kind of candidates was so obtuse that it could not be understood whom it applied to and whether Arywitz was referring to Democratic or Republican candidates.

A special election was soon declared for the Twenty-Seventh Congressional District Seat. After it became obvious that Butchko would not run, national leaders of the AFL-CIO announced that they would make an all-out effort to elect a Democrat to the seat.

On the Saturday after the close of filing for the special election, Butchko visited the offices of the Newhall Signal and spoke with the new editor, Scott Newhall. Scott Newhall said that Butchko's 1968 campaign was a noble effort, and he asked Butchko if there was any way he could get into the special election.

The local AFL-CIO endorsed John Van de Kamp, a former Justice Department lawyer, even before the first special election. There were two Democratic candidates, and ten Republican candidates running, and it was virtually certain that the first special election would be followed by a runoff election. Van de Kamp was opposed to extending the national labor laws to farm workers, and he was opposed to repeal of Section 14B of the national labor law. On both of these important issues, Van de Kamp's positions were contrary to the clear positions of organized labor. In 1968, Van de Kamp had been in charge of the Justice Department's prosecution of Dr. Benjamin Spock for advocating draft resistance. Dr. Spock was convicted, but his conviction was reversed on appeal. Van de Kamp would not have got a conviction of Dr. Spock unless he wanted to.

A special committee organized by the State Central Committee of the Democratic Party endorsed Van de Kamp over the other Democratic candidate before the first special election. State Law prohibited the State Central Committee from endorsing candidates in a primary election, and the first special election to fill a vacancy was similar to a primary election in that there were other Democratic candidates on the ballot. Stephen Reinhardt, who with Jess Unruh's support had become the State Chairman of the California Democratic Party, played an active role in the activities of the special committee. It seemed unusual that Butchko received no notification of the meetings or activities of the special committee.

The Los Angeles Times gave a strong endorsement to Van de Kamp.

Throughout his campaign, Van de Kamp did not express any criticism of the Vietnam War policies of the Nixon administration. Van de Kamp ran as a hawk.

Van de Kamp finished second in the first special election with 13,000 votes. Gary Schlesinger, the California Democratic Council endorsed candidate, received 12,000 votes. Barry Goldwater finished first with 66,000 votes. The runoff election was closer.

On the Sunday before the runoff, Van de Kamp was interviewed on television and he said that he approved of Nixon's Vietnam War policies, which consisted of continuing military pressure in South Vietnam. Nixon was pursuing a military victory.

In his mailer before the runoff, Van de Kamp showed a picture of himself shaking hands with J. Edgar Hoover. J. Edgar Hoover was then known to have said that the anti-Vietnam war movement got its inspiration from outside the United States.

Van de Kamp ran as a hawk in the campaign before the special election and in the campaign before the runoff.

The L.A. Times endorsed Van de Kamp in the runoff. Television station KNXTV, with Jerry Dunphy, endorsed Barry Goldwater, Jr., on the weekend before the runoff election. In the evening of the runoff election, Butchko attended a banquet of the Southern California Association of Defense Counsel. There a lawyer who had been in Butchko's law school class, said to Butchko that unlike Van de Kamp, Butchko had run against an incumbent. At this banquet, a lawyer in Dryden, Harrington and Swartz told Butchko that an attorney in the U.S. Attorney's office in Los Angeles had been campaigning actively for Van de Kamp and had conducted a fundraising event for Van de Kamp. The Hatch Act, the federal corrupt practices law, prohibits this kind of activity.

On the Friday following the runoff in the Twenty-Seventh Council District, Butchko attended a Jefferson Jackson day dinner in Van Nuys. Congressman Corman spoke and said that when Van de Kamp ran for Congress in 1969, there was unity in the Democratic Party in the Twenty-Seventh Congressional District, whereas there was not such unity in 1968. After Corman spoke, State Senator Tom Carrell spoke and said, regarding the Democratic Party, "We fight." Tom Carrell clearly implied that Jim Corman was fighting against Butchko. This statement by Tom Carrell gave a big boost to Butchko and to the cause of peace.

122

On the week after Tom Carrell clearly implied that Jim Corman was fighting against Butchko, the fact that this gave a big boost to Butchko was manifested by Dryden, Harrington and Swartz, giving to Butchko an unsolicited pay raise of $100 a month.

John Mitchell, a trial attorney from San Diego, said you showed us that the country was ready for a revolution.

Under the Nixon Administration, Matt Byrne Jr., a registered Democrat, stayed on as United States Attorney in Los Angeles through all of 1969, and into May of 1970.

In the fall of 1969, a Superior Court Judge in Long Beach named Max Wizot, had occasion to rule on a law and motion question in a case in which Butchk o was working for his law firm. The judge was a Mason, and he reacted in an unusual manner to the legal questions before him.

When Butchko and the attorney for the other party approached the attorneys table for their argument on the question, Judge Wizot said he would not permit any argument on the demurrer to the amendment to the complaint, which amendment had been filed by Butchko.

The judge then said he was striking the amendment to the complaint on his own motion on the grounds that where he grants leave to amend after sustaining a demurrer, it is permissible to file an amended complaint, but it is improper to file an amendment to the complaint as Butchko had done. This ruling was completely contrary to the law as set forth in a California appellate court opinion. Butchko had said nothing to antagonize the judge.

Throughout 1969, the powerful Los Angeles Times gave Jess Unruh tremendous amounts of publicity in advance of his expected race for Governor of California in 1970. Unruh was no longer Speaker of the Assembly but was the Assembly Minority Leader throughout 1969. Unruh took measures to strengthen his control over the Democratic Party in the Twenty-Seventh Congressional District. In late 1969, he chose John Van de Kamp as his campaign manager for the Governor's race.

On the Saturday on which Ted Kennedy had his auto accident at Chappaquiddick, Butchko attended a party for Democrats in the Northeast of the Valley. Butchko spoke with people there and exchanged greetings with Senator Tom Carrell.

In the first part of 1969, members of the Democratic State Central Committee were specially invited to attend a meeting of the Los Angeles County Democratic Central Committee. Butchko attended this meeting.

In about the spring of 1969, Nixon announced that he was withdrawing 50,000 troops from Vietnam by a definite date. Butchko's book describing his campaign for Congress, combined with his political activities were the major factor in bringing about this troop withdrawal.

Nixon always wanted to be in good with Reagan.

In the middle of 1969, Butchko received a letter from Bob Jeans. Bob Jeans had been Alan Cranston's successful campaign manager in 1968. In this letter Bob Jeans offered to manage a campaign for Butchko.

In about the late summer or early fall of 1969, Butchko attended a special program of the Los Angeles County ACLU at USC. At this program, a Black Assemblyman Greene of Los Angeles spoke and said if you are one of the persons being

124

repressed, you could have all of the facts and all of the law on your side and still lose. Butchko had been specially invited to the program by someone who had been in his law school class, a Phillip Chronis, who was then the President of the Los Angeles County Chapter of the ACLU. After this program, Francis E. Jones, a professor at the USC Law School asked Butchko if he was going to run for public office.

Butchko next went to UCLA where he heard a speech by Tom Hayden who complained about the trial of the Chicago Seven, of whom he was one. In this speech Tom Hayden spoke critically of all candidates for public office. Butchko thought that this criticism was unfair to candidates like Butchko.

After this speech, Butchko spoke with an attorney named Kenneth Silk who had been in Butchko's class at the USC Law School. Butchko said to Kenneth Silk something that motivated the Masons to put pressure on Nixon to make a troop withdrawal. Butchko said that John Kennedy was killed by a conspiracy of the Masons.

The following week, Nixon announced that he was going to withdraw another 50,000 troops from Vietnam by a definite date. Butchko's book combined with his political activities were the major factor in bringing about this troop withdrawal.

In December of 1969, Lyndon Johnson said in a nationally televised interview with Walter Cronkite that when he announced his decision not to seek renomination on March 31, 1968, he had been influenced by the McCarthy movement, the young people and other forces at work in the Democratic Party as a result of which it would be difficult for him to continue his policies and maintain peace in the cities at the same time. He also said that he realized it would be a rough political year and that when announced his decision, he knew that Kennedy would have to deal with that problem.

Sometime after this, Johnson stated that he made the second bombing halt of North Vietnam (the small southern portion) on October 31, 1968, because of all the uproar. Most of this uproar was caused by Butchko's aggressive campaign, including his speeches on the war in Vietnam, and his attacks on Reinecke.

Butchko's speeches on the war in Vietnam had the effect of moving the country.

He was still a member of the Democratic State Central Committee of California and would be such until the date of the California primary in June of 1970.

In January of 1970, Butchko opened a law office on Victory Boulevard in Burbank and he became politically active. He attended political meetings and parties in 1970's.

He was still a member of the Democratic State Central Committee of California and would be such until the date of the California primary in June.

Butchko's opening of his own law office at the beginning of 1970 had a tremendous effect on advancing the peace movement throughout 1970.

Since 1968, Butchko was under more surveillance by more people than anyone else. This made Butchko the most effective person in advancing the peace movement.

In January of 1970, Butchko said to Jeanne Caya that in 1968, Butchko and McCarthy were the one-two punch of the peace movement. Jeanne Caya agreed with that statement. Jeanne Caya had been in charge of the main headquarters for McCarthy in the San Fernando Valley. This headquarters had been on Van Nuys Boulevard in Van Nuys.

In January of 1970, Butchko attended a party for Jess Unruh at a hall near downtown Los Angeles. John Van de Kamp was Unruh's campaign manager. He looked surprised to see Butchko. Then campaign signs supporting John Tunney for United

States Senate were taken down in the hall. John Tunney was opposed by George Brown in the Democratic primary.

In January of February of 1970, Butchko appeared at a fundraising party for George Brown at the Music Center in Los Angeles. Butchko discussed his 1968 campaign with the people at his table. Butchko was seen by George Brown.

In about January of 1970, Butchko appeared at a gathering of mostly non-CDC Democrats in Van Nuys. Butchko there spoke with Fred Ball who was running for Assembly in the Sixty-Fourth Assembly District.

In January Butchko attended a huge banquet sponsored by the Glendale and Burbank Bar Associations at a large hall in Burbank. Butchko spoke with some people there including Judge Walters, a respected Municipal Court Judge in Burbank. In 1970 Butchko served on the telephone committee of the Burbank Bar Association.

Throughout 1970, Butchko attended the monthly meetings of the Burbank Bar Association and spoke with people there. Butchko was a member of the Democratic State Central Committee in the first half of 1970.

Butchko mailed out press releases announcing that he would attend the statewide convention of the California Democratic Council in March.

Butchko attended the annual convention of the California Democratic Council held in Fresno in March. Under the California Democratic Council Constitution and by-laws, Butchko's status as a nominee of the Democratic Party in the last general election gave him the right to be an individual delegate both to the statewide California Democratic Council Convention and to the Council of Democratic Clubs for his Congressional District. His attendance as an individual delegate to the California

Democratic Council Convention received publicity in the Burbank Daily Review. Butchko had received his convention call from the office of the California Democratic Council President, John Burton. At the convention, Butchko noticed the presence of John Van de Kamp, who was then acting as Jess Unruh's campaign manager.

Shortly after the statewide convention of the Democratic Party, Butchko attended a party at Travers Devine's home in Burbank. Clyde Bullock was also there. Clyde Bullock was the President of the United Auto Workers of the San Fernando Valley, which worked with the Los Angeles County Federation of Labor on political endorsements. Clyde Bullock said to Butchko, "When you want to run for office see me." Clyde Bullock was in charge of interviewing candidates for endorsement by the Los Angeles County Federation of Labor in the San Fernando Valley. In about March of 1970, Butchko appeared at a meeting of the Twenty-Seventh Congressional District Democratic Council at a hall in Studio City.

In 1970 Travers Devine became the Democratic nominee for assembly in the Sixty-Second Assembly District. He was unopposed in the primary. Throughout 1970, Travers Devine promoted Butchko's political interests. Butchko was certain to be appointed to the Democratic State Central Committee late in 1970.

The Burbank Daily Review published Butchko's press release stating that he would attend the statewide convention of California Democratic Council in Fresno in March of 1970 and describing some of Butchko's background. Butchko's article in the Burbank Daily Review gave a big boost to the peace movement.

128

At the California Democratic Council convention Butchko was seen by Ben Leeds, Anthony Bielenson, and Jess Unruh. Butchko spoke with Ted Lane, Jerry Raskin and Gary Schlesinger and with Vern Bullough, a liberal candidate for the Democratic nomination for Assembly in a district situated in the San Fernando Valley. At the California Democratic Convention, Butchko told Travers Devine and Paul Perlin that Butchko was supporting McGovern for President.

In April and May of 1970 Butchko attended the meetings of the Reseda-West Valley Democratic Club at Ted Lane's house in Canoga Park, and spoke with people there.

Prior to the California Democratic Council convention Joseph Alioto had said that Nixon was exerting tremendous pressure to prevent Alioto from running for the Democratic nomination for Governor against Unruh.

In March Butchko attended a meeting of the Twenty-Seventh Congressional District Democratic Council in Studio City and spoke with people there.

Congressman George Brown was then engaged in a close and hard fought contest with John Tunney for the Democratic nomination to run against California's incumbent Republican Senator George Murphy. At the California Democratic Council convention, George Brown won the delegates' endorsement by an almost unanimous vote. Butchko, who had previously indicated his support for Brown, soon became a member of the Speakers Bureau for George Brown. Brown did not hesitate to point out in his campaign literature that Tunney had in the past supported Johnson's war policies of escalation, and that Tunney had been a member of the Lynch-Johnson delegate slate in 1968

In the first half of 1968, Nixon appointed Jack Howard to the Burbank draft board.

On April 3, Butchko gave a speech on behalf of George Brown's candidacy before a gathering of Democrats in Covina. Butchko attacked Nixon's Vietnam War policies and said that George Brown's victory in California would clearly point the way that the Democratic Party must take for the 1972 Presidential campaign. In this speech, Butchko said that it was necessary to prepare to elect a Democratic peace candidate President in 1972. After Butchko's speech, a gentleman said that we owe a debt of gratitude to the peace candidates of 1968. Butchko's speech in Covina had a tremendous effect on advancing the peace movement.

After this, Butchko's first speech on behalf of George Brown, the next edition of Newsweek states on its cover: "The Presidency, the job that Nixon cannot fill." This action by Newsweek was a result of Butchko's speech, his first since 1968

In April, Butchko attended a party at the home of a California Democratic Council Democrat in the Northwest Valley. At this party, Toni Kimmell spoke as a candidate and made a poor impression. Among other things, she said that she was a violent pacifist. At this party a man told Butchko that Reinecke had been more significant as a Congressman than Barry Goldwater, Jr.

In April Butchko attended a rally for George Brown at a theater or auditorium in downtown Los Angeles. William Shirer spoke in favor of George Brown. Before the speaking began, Butchko spoke with California Democratic Council Democrats from the San Fernando Valley in the lobby. In April, Butchko attended a meeting of the Reseda-West Valley Democratic Club in Canoga Park, and spoke with people there.

130

Butchko's former campaign manager was now running unopposed for the Democratic

Nomination for Assembly in the Sixty-Second Assembly District.

Butchko regularly attended meetings of the Burbank Bar Association in 1970, and he served on the telephone committee of the Bar Association.

In April of 1970, Butchko sent George McGovern a letter in which Butchko stated that he supported McGovern's strong peace positions on Vietnam. McGovern sent Butchko a reply letter thanking Butchko for his support.

Nixon launched an invasion of Cambodia in April of 1970. This action seemed to encounter a tremendous amount of public opposition. On April 29, Travers told Butchko that Butchko had been elected Vice-Chairman of the Twenty-Seventh Congressional District Democratic Council at one of the Council's meetings.

The election of Butchko as Vice-Chairman of the Twenty-Seventh Congressional District Democratic Council gave a big boost to the peace movement. In 1970 Butchko's book made him one of the most powerful persons in the United States. Butchko's working on his book in 1970 put pressure on the Masons to put pressure on Nixon and was thus a major factor in bringing about the troop withdrawal of 150,000 troops from Vietnam announced on May 1, 1970. In 1970, Butchko was under surveillance by a huge number of people.

George Brown was now calling for Nixon's impeachment. On May 1, 1970, Nixon announced that he would withdraw an additional 150,000 troops from Vietnam within a twelve month period and that he would withdraw United States ground troops from Cambodia.

Butchko's working on his book combined with his political activities were the major factor in bringing about this troop withdrawal of 150,000 troops from South Vietnam announced on May 1, 1970.

Butchko's return to active politics in 1970 resulted in a weakening of Nixon's overall strength, and it increased pressure on Nixon to make troop withdrawals. Butchko was the major factor in de-escalating and ending the war in Vietnam. Butchko made all the difference in de-escalating and ending the war in Vietnam.

The fundamental underlying pressure for all the troop withdrawals was created by the cessation of the bombing of North Vietnam in 1968.

In May, Butchko spoke again as a member of George Brown's Speakers Bureau this time before a meeting of the Sunland-Tujunga Democratic Club at the club's headquarters on Foothill Boulevard in Sunland. The lady in George Brown's Speakers Bureau who asked him to give this speech said, "We know that you are popular in that area."

In June, Tunney won the Democratic nomination for the United States Senate. George Brown received a respectable vote. Jess Unruh soon terminated John Van de Kamp's services as his campaign manager.

On June 26, the Valley Green Sheet published an article stating that Travers Devine had appointed John T. Butchko as a co-chairman of the Travers Devine Assembly campaign committee. This article described Butchko as "Burbank attorney, John T. Butchko, vice chairman of the Twenty-Seventh Congressional District Democratic

Council, and a former candidate for Congress." Butchko continued to attend political meetings and parties during the summer.

At a Democratic rally in North Hollywood, Sigmund Arywitz spoke and introduced Fred Ball as the man who was going to carry the Sixty-Fourth Assembly District for the Democratic Party. Arywitz said that we should have been carrying it all along.

In June after the primary Butchko attended a meeting of the Twenty-Seventh Council District Democratic Council. At this meeting Toni Kimmell said, "We all hate Gary Schlesinger."

In the summer of 1970, Butchko attended a party at Tom Carrell's house and yard in the Northeast Valley. Butchko exchanged greeting with Helen Greenberg, a wealthy Valley Democrat, and with Tom Carrell and Congressman Jim Corman. Butchko shook hands with Corman. A man said to Butchko that Jess Unruh's chickens had come home to roost. Butchko spoke with many people there.

In the summer of 1970, Butchko attended a party for Jess Unruh's supporters at Jess Unruh's home in Inglewood. Butchko had been invited in writing to attend this party by Jess Unruh.

In the summer of 1970, Butchko sent Tom Carrell a letter stating Butchko's support for Tom Carrell's re-election campaign. Tom Carrell sent Butchko a reply letter thanking him for his support and stating that he would use his letter of support.

Butchko was required to close his law office on Victory Boulevard at the end of September as a result of his landlord's decision to make his office available to the County

Public Welfare Department, which already occupied most of the office building and was now determined to expand its office space.

Before moving his business to another office in Burbank, Butchko took a vacation in New York City in October. Rumors were then circulated that Butchko would seek to have published a book describing his 1968 campaign for Congress. This seemed to cause some concern and apprehension among some of the Masons and among some of the establishment. When Butchko arrived in New York City, there was an official announcement that Nixon would withdraw 10,000 or 20,000 troops from Vietnam by a date ahead of a previously scheduled date.

Butchko returned to Burbank in time to observe the final stages of the general election campaign in California.

In 1969, Congressman Barry Goldwater, Jr. had crashed his airplane onto a house in the San Fernando Valley and this made him a weaker candidate for re-election.

At the beginning of November, Butchko opened a law office on Magnolia Boulevard in Burbank. Butchko then wrote to Senator George McGovern stating that he was considering offering support for George McGovern should McGovern become a Presidential candidate. McGovern replied, thanking Butchko for his offer of support.

In November of 1970, Barry Goldwater, Jr., defeated Toni Kimmell by a margin of about 60,000 votes.

Californians exhibited a high degree of split ticket voting. The Democrat Tunney won a Senate seat from George Murphy. Murphy had been severely handicapped by a voice problem. As a result of surgery during his term in office he had been left with a voice that sounded like a loud rasping whisper. Murphy was probably not electable against any Democrat in 1970. Edmund G. Brown, Jr., a son of the former Governor won election to the office of Secretary of State by a small margin over a Black Republican. Reagan, Reinecke and the other Republican statewide candidates all won by large margins. Reagan won by over 900,000 votes. The Democrats won a narrow margin of seats in the State Legislature. Experts had never expected Jess Unruh to win the governorship at any time throughout the year. But in the last month of the campaign the Reagan lead seemed to decline from over a million votes (as projected in a New York Times article) to about 600,000 when Nixon did several surprising things: He declared that the 1970 election would amount to a referendum of his policies on the war in Vietnam. He came to California to take an active part in the Republican campaigns although Reagan's expected victory margin indicated that Republican candidates were already running about as strong as they could on a state where the ratio of registered Democrats to registered Republicans was about three to two. In Northern California, Nixon flashed a peace sign to a group of anti-war demonstrators and encountered an angry and allegedly disorderly response. Nixon then made new appeals for law and order.

Law and order did seem to be a paramount topic of discussion by candidates generally in that general election campaign. George Murphy stressed law and order, and Tunney did also but to a lesser degree. Edmund G. Brown, Jr. emphasized law and order and the dangers from political militants.

In November of 1970, the Republicans lost eleven state governorships and ten seats in the House of Representatives.

For several weeks following the November general elections, there were rumors that Nixon was planning to escalate the war in Vietnam.

Butchko soon put a sign on the front of his office and began attending political meetings. The very visible sign on Butchko's new office quickly gained increased interest in his political activities.

Nixon did not escalate the war in Vietnam. Butchko put on the wall of his office his framed Master of Laws diploma.

In November of 1970, after the general election, Butchko attended a meeting of the Twenty-Seventh Congressional District Democratic Council at a home in the West Valley. At this meeting Butchko told Ted Lane, the mainstay of the Reseda-West Valley Democratic Club, that he was supporting George McGovern for President.

Throughout Butchko told Congressional Democratic Council club members that he was supporting McGovern for President at meetings and parties of the Twenty-Seventh Congressional District Democratic Council and its affiliated clubs.

Butchko had a great lease for his store front office on Magnolia Boulevard. It started for the first year on November 1, 1970, for a monthly rent of $105, and it could be renewed by Butchko each year for another year up to a total of five years, and the monthly rent would increase by only five dollars for each renewal of the lease. Thus in the fifth year of the lease (assuming Butchko renewed) the rent would be only $125 per month.

Reinecke was elected Lieutenant Governor by about 957,000 votes – larger than the margin of victory for other victorious Republicans for statewide office including Reagan. Butchko gained a tremendous amount of power and prestige because Reinecke had now defeated a member of the Democratic establishment, State Senator Alfred Alquist, by 957,000 votes.

In about December of 1970, Travers Devine appointed Butchko to membership on the Democratic State Central Committee of California for the term from January 1, of 1971 to December 31, 1972. Butchko's appointment to the Democratic State Central Committee received some newspaper coverage in the Valley Green Sheet, in the San Fernando Valley Section of the Los Angeles Times, and in the Glendale Independent. This was Butchko's second consecutive term on the Democratic State Central Committee. The articles announcing Butchko's appointment to the Democratic State Central Committee also stated that Butchko was an attorney in Burbank and that in 1968 he had won the Democratic nomination for Congress in the Twenty-Seventh Congressional District.

Butchko made all the difference in de-escalating and ending the war in Vietnam.

In December of 1970, George Brown sent Butchko a letter in which he said that working with Butchko was one of the most constructive experiences he had in 1970.

In December of 1970, Butchko received a letter from Chuck Manatt in which he said that he knew that Butchko had earned his appointment to the Democratic State Central Committee by hard work.

Robert Moretti became the Speaker of the Assembly in 1971. Toni Kimmell seemed determined to continue to play a leading role in the Twenty-Seventh Congressional District. At a meeting of the Twenty-Seventh Congressional District Democratic Council in Sunland in December of 1970, Toni incorrectly stated that Butchko was not a delegate to the Council. Butchko pointed out that under the California

137

Democratic Council Constitution and By-Laws, he was both an individual member of the California Democratic Council and an individual delegate to the California Democratic Council and would continue to be such until December 31, 1972, which was the last date of the Congressional term for which he had been nominated.

Travers was seeking to convert the Twenty-Seventh Congressional District Democratic Council into a new San Fernando Valley Council in order to increase the membership and to get new opportunities for publicity. Toni led the opposition to this effort. She asserted that it could not be done under the California Democratic Council Constitution and by-laws. The issue came to a head at an exciting meeting at Ted Lane's home in Canoga Park in January. Travers' motion to change the Council was voted down.

At this meeting, Toni stated that Butchko was not even a member of any affiliated club. This was, of course, untrue. Butchko was indeed a member of the Reseda-West Valley Democratic Club. He was not only a member of a Club, but he was also an individual delegate to the Council by virtue of his membership on the Democratic State Central Committee. The by-laws of the California Democratic Council provided that members of the State Central Committee were individual delegates to the Council for the district in which they resided.

In January of 1971, Butchko became aware that Butchko was under video surveillance in his home and office and other places where he was known to be.

Butchko's being under surveillance by more people than anyone else made Butchko tremendously powerful in advancing the peace movement and made Butchko the most effective person in advancing the peace movement.

138

George McGovern announced in January of 1971 that he would be a candidate for President. Butchko immediately sent McGovern a letter assuring him of Butchko's support, and then received a letter from McGovern thanking him for his support. McGovern also stated in this letter that: "With your continued support, we will win."

Butchko was then planning to run for Congress against Barry Goldwater, Jr., in 1972, and he decided to begin active preparations for this early in 1971. The redistricting which was expected to take place in 1971 would probably change the district considerably. But Butchko calculated that the district would probably not be made much more difficult for a Democrat because it had already been gerrymandered in 1967 to give some degree of safety to a Republican incumbent, and Congressmen from adjoining districts who had also been protected by the 1967 gerrymandering would probably not want radical changes in their districts.

In January, a spirited contest was developing between George Brown and Charles "Chuck" Manatt for election to the post of State Chairman of the Democratic Party. Manatt was an attorney in Van Nuys and the President of the San Fernando Valley Bar Association. In 1969, Manatt had been an unsuccessful candidate for election to the Los Angeles Community College Board of Trustees. Manatt was a political associate of Jim Corman and Bob Moretti. In contrast with George Brown, Manatt had never been elected to public office.

Butchko endorsed George Brown and received significant publicity for this.

In the middle of January of 1971, the Burbank Daily Review, the Burbank News, and the Glendale News Press all published articles stating that: "John T. Butchko

139

announced today that he endorses George Brown for state chairman of the Democratic State Central Committee of California.

"Butchko is an attorney in Burbank. He has served as a member of the Los Angeles County Democratic Central Committee and as a member of the Democratic State Central Committee of California."

"He is presently a member of the Democratic State Central Committee."

"In 1968, Butchko won the Democratic nomination for Congress in the Twenty-Seventh Congressional District".

The Burbank News was delivered to every residence in Burbank.

In December of 1970, shortly before the meeting of the Democratic State Central Committee, Butchko attended a party at the home of a Democrat in Burbank; Travers Devine and Lesley Chambers were there. Butchko told people there that he was running for Congress in the Twenty-Seventh Congressional District. Lesley Chambers, Travers' girlfriend, asked Butchko what he was running for this time. Butchko said: "For principles."

The meeting of the Democratic State Central Committee took place in Sacramento on the weekend of January 23 and 24. Some committee meetings and parties were held on Friday, January 22. Butchko attended the party for George Brown. George Brown was there and told Butchko that he looked better than he did. Attendance was heavy at the party for George Brown, and it looked as though he had a good chance of wining.

The members of the State Committee within each Congressional District were entitled to elect one man and one woman, to serve as co-chairman of the District

140

delegation and as members of the Executive Board of the State Central Committee. On Saturday afternoon, January 23, Butchko sought election to that position at the caucus of State Central Committee members for the Twenty-Seventh District. He was supported by Travers Devine, Lesley Chambers, and Nettie Baker, a leader of the Sunland-Tujunga Democratic Club, who had been appointed to the State Committee by Travers.

Butchko was opposed for the office by Fred Ball and by William Bluestein, an attorney who had been appointed to the State Committee by Toni Kimmell. Toni was seeking re-election to the post also and she was leading the opposition to Butchko.

In a statement on behalf of his candidacy, Butchko said, among other things, that if

elected to the post, he would work to unite every element in the Democratic Party that was willing to work for the common goal, the defeat of the Nixon Administration. The caucus elected Bluestein to the post. Butchko received four votes; Fred Ball got four votes. Travers said that Toni Kimmell's activities had defeated Butchko.

Senator Muskie addressed the members of the State Committee at a Saturday afternoon banquet. Senator McGovern addressed the State Committee members at a banquet on Saturday evening.

McGovern was introduced by Senator Cranston, who said that McGovern was the "leader of the war to end the war in the Senate." Among other things, McGovern said that the Democrats had lost the Presidential election of 1968 as a result of the war in Vietnam. He told the Committee members that it was time to elect a Democratic President and to stop the destruction of Democrats.

On Sunday, Senator Birch Bayh of Indiana addressed the State Committee as a potential presidential candidate. He criticized wiretapping and said that there was no place for any police tactic in the United States.

George Brown got the largest number of votes on the first ballot. Manatt was a close second. Leon Cooper, the former State Chairman of the Democratic Party, who had support from labor members of the State Committee finished third. Sigmund Arywitz was present and attempted to provide leadership for the labor committeemen. On the second ballot, most of Leon Cooper's votes went to Manatt, and Manatt narrowly defeated Brown. Jim Corman had been one of the pro-Manatt workers who actively solicited support for Manatt on the Convention floor.

After the meeting of the State Committee, Butchko received a letter from Birch Bayh stating that Senator Bayh was pleased to have had Butchko present at his hospitality breakfast on a day of the meeting of the State Committee. Senator Birch Bayh of Indiana was running for President of the United States.

The events of this meeting of the State Central Committee seemed significant to Butchko, and they seemed to provide some grounds for a reassessment of the entire political situation, especially as it affected his chances for winning a Congressional seat.

It seemed that Butchko's overall political reputation was rather good in 1971. After all, the only man who had defeated him in an election was Ed Reinecke, a Republican, who subsequently in 1970 had defeated a Democratic State Senator to win the Lieutenant Governorship of California by a larger margin of votes than any other candidate for statewide office in 1970.

On the other hand, Moretti's acquisition of the Speakership of the Assembly, established a major power in Butchko's own general area of the San Fernando Valley. Moretti had been accustomed to aligning himself with Jim Corman and with conservative Democrats along with the conservative leaders of organized labor. Moretti was now in a powerful position to determine the boundaries of the Twenty-Seventh Congressional District. In general, the defeat of Jess Unruh and his removal from the speakership seemed to provide new opportunities for new young Democratic members of the State Legislature to achieve more power for themselves. Unruh's tremendous power had tended to limit the power of all the other Democrats in the Legislature on a more or less equal basis.

In 1970, when Reinecke won the general election for Lieutenant Governor over State Senator Alfred Alquist, a member of the Democratic Party establishment, by 957,000 votes, this tremendously increased Butchko's power and prestige.

Butchko seemed to gain a more favorable position after the State Central Committee meeting. Butchko believed that McGovern and Bayh's speeches indicated that the national Democratic Party would be going quite liberal in 1972 and that should be favorable for Butchko. McGovern's exhortation against the destruction of Democrats had pleased Butchko. Although he had not regarded himself as destroyed, the activities of leading Democrats in regard to the Twenty-Seventh Congressional District and the ascendancy of Moretti and Manatt in Butchko's general area had seemed to come close to putting some limitations on Butchko's power.

Nonetheless, throughout 1971, most of the members of the Twenty-Seventh Congressional District and its affiliated Clubs regarded Butchko as the front-runner for the Democratic nomination for Congress in that district.

At a meeting of the Twenty-Seventh Congressional District Democratic Council following the State Central Committee meeting, Nancy Lund, the President of the Sunland-Tujunga Democratic Club, stated that George Brown had recently spoken to her club and said that Moretti had called the Democratic members of the Legislature and told them that if they did not vote for Manatt they would not be appointed to legislative committees. Toni Kimmell now stopped asserting that Butchko was not a delegate to the Council, and it was officially acknowledged that he was indeed an individual delegate. Butchko attended this Council meeting.

Chuck Manatt now established an openly friendly relationship with George Brown, who was eager to run for re-election to Congress in a new district where a Democrat could win.

On March 14, a large "Friends of Manatt" was held at the Sportsman's Lodge, with Corman and Moretti as sponsor. Corman said that Manatt won the post of State Chairman because he took his case to his peers, and he said that Moretti became speaker of the Assembly "because he has the capacity to be the Speaker." Before the dinner, Butchko saw Toni Kimmell talking with Jim Corman. Toni was telling Corman of the work she was doing in Santa Monica in preparation for the California Democratic Council Convention there on the weekend of April 2-4. Manatt told Butchko that he was welcome to the dinner.

Throughout 1971 Butchko attended all of the meetings of the Twenty-Seventh Congressional District Democratic Council and all of the meetings of the Reseda-West Valley Democratic Club and most of the meetings of the Sunland-Tujunga Democratic Club, and all of the meetings of the San Fernando Valley Democratic Council, and all the parties of the Reseda-West Valley Democratic Club, and all the parties of the Sunland-Tujunga Democratic Club.

Throughout 1971, Butchko attended all of the meetings of the Burbank Bar Association. These were monthly meetings. Butchko continued to serve as a member of the telephone committee of the Burbank Bar Association.

Butchko attended the California Democratic Council Convention as an alternate. Alternates sat with delegates and so the status did not make much practical difference. Toni Kimmell was unopposed for the position of Vice-Chairman (Chairman) for the Southern Region of the California Democratic Council. Toni presided over portions of the Saturday banquet. George McGovern spoke to the Convention. Moretti and Manatt spoke to the convention. Fred Ball also attended this convention and he could be seen lending support to Toni. George Brown had been asked by many to seek the California Democratic Council Chairmanship, but he declined.

A blackman, Nate Holden, was unopposed for the Chairmanship. He had done a lot of work for the California Democratic Council, and he was generally regarded as a sincere California Democratic Council type liberal. McGovern's appearance at this convention was very impressive political activity, since McGovern was already seeking support for his campaign for the Democratic Presidential nomination. At a hospitality party during the convention, Butchko met and shook hands with Birch Bayh, who was a Senator from Indiana.

On the last day of the California Democratic Council Convention, Butchko's father, an astute political observer, told Butchko that he was far ahead of Toni Kimmell in popular support for the Democratic nomination for Congress in the Twenty-Seventh Congressional District. On that date, Nixon announced that he was withdrawing 50,000 more troops from Vietnam by a definite date. Butchko's emergence as the front runner for the Democratic nomination for Congress in the Twenty-Seventh Congressional District was the major factor in bringing about this troop withdrawal.

After the California Democratic Council Convention, Jerry Brown endorsed Muskie for President.

Shortly after the California Democratic Convention, Butchko reported on the new by-laws at a meeting of the Burbank Bar Association. Butchko had participated with Mr. Montgomery, the President of the Burbank Bar Association, in preparing these by-laws. At a joint meeting of the Burbank and Glendale Bar Associations, Mr. Montgomery had praised Butchko's work in preparing these by-laws.

Throughout the remainder of 1971, Butchko continued to be the front runner for the Democratic nomination for Congress. But Butchko would be a major target for many of the more serous hawks.

Travers Devine along with Lesley Chambers and Irv Katz now formed a public relations firm known as Election Direction Associates. Travers was trying to become a professional campaign manager, and he became a Southern California chairman of the Fred Harris Presidential Campaign, and when Harris dropped out of the race, Travers became a Southern California Chairman of the Vance Hartke campaign. While Travers continued to support Butchko for the California Democratic Council endorsement in the Twenty-Seventh Congressional District, the campaign management services were now unavailable to Butchko, who was supporting McGovern for President.

Chuck Manatt with the backing of top members of the Democratic establishment in California was promoting a so-called Democratic Party Reform Plan. This plan would change the existing party organization consisting of county committees and the state committee, into a pyramidal hierarchy of organizations, some of which would have the power to make official pre-primary endorsements of candidates. The California Democratic Council was always opposed to official pre-primary endorsement of candidates. Opponents of the Manatt plan charged that it would lead to Eastern-style politics. The plan would have required a huge overhaul of state election laws and procedures in that it called for election of some party officials in special districts consisting of only five precincts each.

Many California Democratic Council Club members vehemently opposed the so-called Party Reform Plan on the grounds that it would tend to supplant the California Democratic Council and that the new structure would be subservient to the Democratic Party establishment. Manat saw fit to call a special convention on Party reforms consist of all the members of the Democratic State Central Committee in addition to special delegates elected at congressional district caucuses open to all Democrats.

The caucus in the Twenty-Seventh Council District was held at the UAW Union Hall in Van Nuys. It was presided over by Toni Kimmell and Bill Bluestein, and was heavily attended. Butchko was a delegate. In speaking on behalf of his own successful candidacy for delegate to the special convention, Ted Lane praised Butchko as our great and glorious candidate of 1968.

While opposing Manatt's Party reform, Gerald Hill, the 1967-68 Chairman of the California Democratic Council, and a political ally of Travers Devine, was promoting a counter plan calling for the election of the members of the State Central Committee to replace the appointment procedures. Travers arranged to have Butchko listed in writing as an official sponsor of the Hill plan at the special convention in San Jose on the weekend of May 14-16. The sponsor's list was a short list. Butchko received excellent publicity (his press release) in the Valley Green Sheet announcing his attendance at this convention.

Butchko enjoyed this convention. He renewed his acquaintance with Marianna VanDerNerf, one of Toni's appointees to the State Committee. Marianna told Butchko that she remembered his speech in Ridgecrest at the candidate's forum sponsored by the Indian Wells Valley League of Women voters in the 1968 general election campaign, and that she thought it was the best speech given on that occasion.

The convention voted for the Democratic Party Reform Plan except for the pre-primary endorsement feature. The Hill plan was defeated. Toni Kimmell seemed to have antagonized some people when she repeatedly interrupted Les Rivers, the Chairman of the Los Angeles County Democratic Central, while he was conducting discussions at a dinner and caucus of delegates from Los Angeles County. Toni insisted on making a big issue over the County Committees' recent endorsement of David Roberti over another Democrat in a special election for a State Senate seat, and went on talking in spite of Les Rivers mightiest efforts to regain the floor.

The Democratic Party Reform Plan was never considered seriously for enactment into law by the State legislature, and so it died.

After this special convention, Butchko continued with his plans to run for Congress in 1972. He wrote to Tom Carrell asking for his support. In a reply letter, Tom stated that he was happy that Butchko would run and that he looked forward to capturing the Twenty-Seventh Council District for the Democratic Party in 1972.

Throughout 1971, Butchko was regarded as the front runner for the Democratic nomination for Congress in the Twenty-Seventh Congressional District by most of the members of the California Democratic Council Clubs in that district.

On the day of the Ali-Frazier fight in 1971, Butchko appeared at a party given by Jim Keysor, a Democratic Assemblyman from the San Fernando Valley. This party was at the Budweiser Brewery in Van Nuys. At the party Butchko spoke with Senator Tom Carrell's field representative. He told Butchko that Toni Kimmell was still speaking and fighting against the man that she had narrowly defeated in the Primary in the Twenty-Seventh Congressional District in 1970.

On June 17, Butchko attended a wine tasting party in Sherman Oaks, which was attended by a large number of Democrats. Butchko spoke with people there.

In the summer, Butchko attended a Sunday afternoon party at the yard of a California Democratic Council Democrat in the West Valley. At this party, Butchko told Assemblyman Allen Sieroty that Butchko was supporting McGovern for President; Butchko spoke with other people there and said that he was supporting McGovern.

On July 10, Butchko attended a party of the Reseda-West Valley Democratic Club in Chatsworth. Butchko spoke with people there. On July 25th, he attended an art

149

exhibit and auction in Encino sponsored by the Fair Housing Council of the San Fernando Valley. A lady in charge of this auction said to Butchko that she knew he was active in politics.

In the summer of 1971, Nixon appointed John Van de Kamp to be the Chief of the Federal Public Defenders Office in Los Angeles.

In the summer of 1971, Senator Birch Bayh sent to Butchko two pictures of Butchko shaking hands with Birch Bayh during a California Democratic Council convention earlier in the year. These pictures said, "My best personal regards to John Butchko, Birch Bayh," and "All good wishes to John, a great Democrat. Birch Bayh."

Butchko had these pictures framed and put them on display in his office, where they stayed for many years and were seen by people in surveillance of Butchko.

In the late summer of 1971, Butchko attended a party for Fred Harris, who was running for the Democratic Presidential nomination. This party was at a hotel hall on Ventura Boulevard. This party was heavily attended by Democrats. Fred Harris exchanged greetings and shook hands with John Butchko and smiled. Butchko spoke with people there.

On August 14th, Butchko attended a party attended by Alan Cranston and many leading Democrats in Studio City. Butchko and Cranston exchanged greetings, and Butchko spoke with people there.

On Sunday, September 12th, the Valley Green Sheet published one of Butchko's press releases in its Burbank edition. It was stated therein that Butchko was an attorney in Burbank and a member of the Democratic State Central Committee and that Butchko was supporting Senator George McGovern for the Democratic nomination for President. Butchko mailed a copy of this press release to McGovern.

In the summer of 1971, Butchko attended a victory party for David Roberti celebrating Roberti's victory in a special election. This party was in Hollywood. Butchko spoke with people there including Travers Devine.

On Friday, September 24, George McGovern made a major speech to a large crowd at the Los Angeles Convention Center. When requests were made for donations, Toni Kimmell declared aloud that she would give $100.00. John Burton, who was conducting the program at that point, said that she was running for Congress, and should not be giving money. Later Toni would oppose McGovern's bid for the California Democratic Council endorsement. After his speech, Butchko and McGovern exchanged greetings, and Butchko said that he was John Butchko. McGovern said to Butchko that it had been a great crowd there, and Butchko agreed. At this time there were very few members of the Democratic establishment in California who were supporting McGovern. There were no Congressmen among his supporters. Muskie then had the most support among the Democratic establishment, and his support among the Democratic establishment would increase during the remainder of 1971.

But Butchko steadfastly supported McGovern, and McGovern did get enough publicity to be a potential contender for the California primary of 1972.

Shortly after McGovern's September speech in Los Angeles, he sent a letter to Butchko in which he said that the support of party regulars was important to his candidacy and that he deeply appreciated Butchko's early endorsement.

In October, Butchko attended a dinner party put on by Joe McGhee in Woodland Hills. Joe was already an announced candidate for the Democratic nomination for State Senator in the Twenty-Third State Senate District in the San Fernando Valley. Joe would continue to be the only apparent candidate for this office until the time of filing for office in 1972.

At this party, Butchko talked some things over with Kent Corey, a writer for a singles publication and a vice-president of a club called the San Fernando Valley Democratic Association, a non-California Democratic Council Club. Corey was about the same age as Butchko and was considering running for Congress also in the Twenty-Seventh Congressional District. When Corey said something about the Twenty-Seventh Congressional District, Lesley Chambers, who was then Travers Devine's wife, said that Butchko was the most beautiful candidate.

On Sunday, October 24th or 31st, Butchko attended a meeting of the Sunland-Tujunga Democratic Club at Nancy Lund's house in Sunland. The meeting involved a discussion of issues and preparation of proposed issues positions for a forthcoming issues conference to be sponsored by the California Democratic Council and other groups. Butchko proposed a resolution calling for a guaranteed minimum income including incentives to work, and a resolution calling for price controls. During the discussion of foreign policy, Butchko proposed a resolution calling on the next Democratic Administration to conduct a governmental investigation of the real reasons why Nixon had prolonged the war in Vietnam. Immediately after this meeting there seemed to be quite a stir in the Los Angeles and national media areas about the war issue. There was an increase in pro-Butchko signals in the media after this meeting. Shortly after this

152

meeting, Nixon officially announced that he would withdraw 50,000 more troops from Vietnam by a definite date. Butchko brought about this troop withdrawal.

On November 5, Butchko attended a party for Congressman Tom Rees at a home in Sherman Oaks. Butchko exchanged greetings with Tom Rees and said that at Helen Greenberg's party in 1967, Tom had told Butchko that Tom was dovish, but that Congress was mostly hawkish. Tom said that he expected that his district would include Studio City and Sherman Oaks after the redistricting.

But it was not certain whether the redistricting would be accomplished as planned in the legislature, and whether Governor Reagan would sign the redistricting bill.

Tom said he was supporting Muskie and that if elected; Muskie would retire the wiretapers to civilian life. Butchko thought that this statement was hyperbole. Since 1968 there was much peace sentiment in the surveillance network.

On November 13, Butchko made some further contributions to the proposed issues positions of the Sunland-Tujunga Democratic Club at a meeting in Sunland.

Butchko received some publicity in the Valley Green Sheet for his attendance at the Issues Conference sponsored by the California Democratic Council and other groups at the International Hotel in Inglewood on November 19, 20 and 21.

Martin Stone, a prominent businessman, spoke there and said that Nixon had created a police state, and that Ed Davis had helped Nixon do it. Ed Davis was the police chief of the City of Los Angeles.

Gerald Hill was at the conference and indicated a favorable view toward Vance Hartke, who spoke at the conference. Butchko spoke with people at the conference.

Senator Henry Jackson of Washington was also emerging as a significant candidate for the Democratic nomination for President at this time. Senator Jackson supported the war in Vietnam.

In October and November, Butchko helped form the Burbank-Glendale McGovern for President Committee along with Ann Segal, and Butchko became a co-chairman of the committee.

On November 29, Butchko attended a planning meeting for the McGovern delegate selection caucus for the Twenty-Seventh Congressional District at Jo Seidita's home in Northridge. Jo Seidita appointed Butchko chairman of the by-laws committee and she said that she knew that Butchko could do that (prepare by-laws).

On November 30, Butchko attended a meeting of the Knights of Columbus in Burbank.

In about November, Butchko attended a large California Democratic Council party at a large home on the West side of Los Angeles. Butchko spoke with people there and exchanged greetings with Senator Mike Gravel of Alaska. Someone at this party said that he or she saw an article in the Valley Publications newspaper stating that John Butchko and Toni Kimmell looked like candidates.

In November or early December of 1971, Butchko attended an outdoors party of Democrats in the central San Fernando Valley. Alan Cranston spoke there. Butchko spoke with people there. One man said to Butchko that it would be nice if the legislature would put a new Congressional district in the San Fernando Valley.

In about November, Mildred Simon called Butchko at his home to ask about a political matter. She was the California Democratic Council endorsed peace candidate

154

against Jim Corman in the 1968 primary. Butchko told her that he was going to run against Barry Goldwater, Jr. She said: "That's good. There has to be some change."

In December, Butchko was eagerly waiting to see if there would be a re-districting and what it would be. In December, Senator Tunney endorsed Muskie. McGovern said that Tunney's endorsement would make a difference of one vote.

In December Butchko attended a meeting of a club called the San Fernando Valley Democratic Association at Helen Greenberg's house in Van Nuys. Butchko exchanged greetings with Tom Carrell's field representative at this meeting.

On December 22, Butchko joined the Sunland-Tujunga Democratic Club in a walk for peace on Foothill Boulevard.

In December Butchko attended a party at Helen Greenberg's house in Van Nuys and spoke with people there including Tom Carrell's field representative.

On December 29, Butchko met with Brian Kovsky, who was now working for the Valley View, a newspaper in the West Valley. Butchko hired Brian to be his campaign manager.

In the latter part of 1971, Butchko attended a meeting at the Burbank-Glendale McGovern for President Committee and spoke with people there.

Butchko attended the Christmas party at Richard Rogan's home in December and spoke with people there.

Butchko then received publicity in the Los Angeles Times, San Fernando Valley Section, announcing that he would appear at a party at the San Fernando Democratic Council in North Hollywood. This party was held at Toni Kimmell's home. Butchko spoke with people there.

155

Corey announced his candidacy for Congress in the Twenty-Seventh Congressional District in December of 1971, and on December 22, Corey's announcement with his background and activities was published in the Valley Publications. Corey soon made the mistake of mailing a letter to active Democrats such as Butchko, in which Corey listed as his local coordinators certain persons who were not in fact supporting Corey and who soon protested.

In December Butchko attended a party of the Sunland-Tujunga Democratic Club. Butchko spoke with people there, including Bill Graham, a member of the Los Angeles County Democratic Central Committee. Bill Graham asked Butchko where Toni Kimmell had gone wrong in her 1978 race against Goldwater, Jr. Butchko told people there, including Bill Graham that Butchko was going to run against Barry Goldwater, Jr. in 1972.

Governor Reagan vetoed the legislature's redistricting plans for the Assembly, State Senate and Congressional seats, all on the grounds that they were gerrymanderers to protect the incumbents. The redistricting, if any, would now be done by the California Supreme Court unless the Court determined that the Governor's veto was not valid.

In January Butchko awaited the Court's decision on redistricting, but he ordered his campaign bumper stickers before he formally announced; the situation called for a difficult decision as to when to announce. This was because Corey was already an announced candidate, while Butchko wanted to see where the district was definitely going to before he made his final decision to announce his candidacy. Brian noted this problem and suggested that Butchko announce before the Court made its decision on reapportionment.

156

On January 9, 1972, Butchko attended a party given by the Sunland McGovern Committee in Sunland. On January 10, he attended a meeting of the San Fernando Valley Democratic Council in Encino.

On January 11, Butchko attended a meeting of the Los Angeles County Democratic Central Committee. At this meeting he was elected to fill a vacancy in the Sixty-Second Assembly District's delegation to the County Committee. This was a major victory. It was announced to entire County Committee that Butchko was appointed to the Committee. A woman at this meeting told Butchko that she still had his campaign literature from 1968.

On January 12, 1972, Butchko mailed to all the newspapers in the district and to radio stations and other media, press releases announcing his appointment to the Los Angeles County Democratic Central Committee. On the evening of January 13, Butchko spoke to the Sunland-Tujunga Democratic Club as a candidate for Congress against Barry Goldwater, Jr. Right after this speech, Nixon announced that he would withdraw another 50,000 troops from Vietnam by a definite date. Butchko brought about this troop withdrawal. In his speech, Butchko said that he planned to conduct an aggressive campaign to unseat Barry Goldwater, Jr. He attacked the Vietnam War policies of the Nixon Administration. He said that in 1972 the club would have an opportunity to work within the political process to bring about a complete disengagement of all our military forces from Vietnam. Butchko also urged continued support for McGovern in his speech at this meeting.

On Saturday, January 15, Butchko met with State Senator Tom Carrell at the Senator's office in San Fernando. Butchko said that he was going to run against Barry

157

Goldwater, Jr., but that he had postponed his formal announcement pending the Court's decision on redistricting. If the Court upheld the Governor's veto, it is possible that the States districts would remain intact. On the other hand, the legislatures redistricting plan would place the Twenty-Seventh Congressional District in the West Valley including Woodland Hills, Tarzana and Encino, Canoga Park, Chatsworth, Northridge, Granada Hills, portions of Reseda, and a portion of Sherman Oaks, and would extend the district into portions of Ventura County to include Oxnard and Port Hueneme. Butchko asked for the Senator's views: Tom, who had encouraged Butchko to run in 1968, encouraged him to run again. Tom said that Butchko might as well announce right away. Tom noted that one need not live in the District where he runs for Congress. Tom Carrell also said that he would support Butchko.

Immediately after his meeting with Tom Carrell, Butchko noted that his support, including signals in the media, increased tremendously.

On January 16, 1972, the Valley Green Sheet published on page 9 in all its editions Butchko's press release announcing his appointment to the County Committee, together with his picture. This article gave Butchko's background, including the fact that he had been an associate editor of the Southern California Law Review, and a research attorney for the United States District Court for the Southern District of California. This article stated that Butchko was an attorney in Burbank, an active member of numerous civic organizations, also a member of the Democratic State Central Committee. The article also stated that in 1968 Butchko had won the Democratic nomination for Congress in the Twenty-Seventh Congressional District. A similar article was published in the

Glendale Ledger and Burbank Ledger on Wednesday, January 19. The Glendale Ledger was delivered to most residences in Glendale.

On Tuesday, January 18, 1972, Butchko mailed press releases formally announcing his candidacy to all the newspapers in the old Twenty-Seventh Congressional District and in the new Twenty-Seventh Congressional District as outlined in the legislature's redistricting plan. Subsequently on January 19, the California Supreme Court made its decision on redistricting. The Court upheld the Governor's veto of the legislature's Assembly and State Senate seats, but the Court said that the Congressional District's had to be redistricted, and it ordered into effect the legislature's plan for redistricting. Reagan and Reinecke vigorously criticized the latter part of the Court's decision. Butchko was prepared to run in either the old Twenty-Seventh Congressional District or in the new Twenty-Seventh Congressional District. As a result of the Court's decision it would be the new Twenty-Seventh Congressional District.

The new district had a higher Democratic registration. Democrats were about 54% of the registered voters in the new district. Butchko thought he would have a good chance to win the Congressional seat in the new district. But Butchko now lived outside the district. The new Twenty-Seventh District had Barry Goldwater, Jr., as the incumbent. Butchko had been the Democratic nominee for Congress in large portions of the West Valley in 1968, including Canoga Parka, Winnetka, Chatsworth, Northridge, Granada Hills, Porter Ranch and some of the northern portion of Woodland Hills. He had recently been active in the Reseda-West Valley Democratic Club.

Since the new Twenty-Seventh District had a higher Democratic registration percentage it was more possible that there might be additional candidates.

159

On Friday, January 21, Butchko attended an Installation of Officers dinner of the Reseda-West Valley Democratic Club at Francois Restaurant in Encino. Tom Bradley was the guest speaker, and there was a good attendance. Brian made Butchko's campaign bumper stickers available at this party. Butchko and Corey were both scheduled to be introduced as candidates for Congress in the Twenty-Seventh Congressional District. Butchko was introduced as a candidate, but Corey seemed to have been bothered by something and he left early. A straw vote showed that most of those in attendance preferred McGovern for the Democratic presidential nomination. Irv Katz, as associate of Traver's public relations firm, became the new president of the Reseda-West Valley Democratic Club. Joe McGhee and Michael Duberchin, Traver's candidate for Assembly in the Fifty-Seventh Assembly District were also in attendance.

On Sunday, January 23, Brian began to do some sniping with Butchko's bumper stickers in some West Valley areas. Also on Sunday, January 23, Butchko began to snipe with his bumper stickers on bus benches without advertising. From January 24 to January 29, Butchko sniped for at least four hours every night, and by Saturday, the 29th, he had done at tremendous amount of sniping throughout the West Valley, and along all of heavily traveled Ventura Boulevard and also on heavily traveled San Fernando Valley streets outside the district, where much of the traffic came to and from the district. Butchko was the first candidate to snipe in the San Fernando Valley in 1972. In those days, there were more bus benches without advertising than there are currently.

On Monday, January 31, Butchko and Brian attended a meeting of the Twenty-Seventh California Democratic Council in Studio City. Now as at many future appearances, Butchko made his bumper stickers available. All in all, January had been a month of success for Butchko's campaign.

McGovern now grew steadily stronger in his campaign for the Democratic nomination for President, and he received increased publicity. Throughout 1971, McGovern had usually got about 4% in polls of Democrats. At the start of January 1972, McGovern had about 4% in the polls.

Butchko's announcement of candidacy had been published in the Ventura County Star-Free Press following a brief telephone interview with one of that newspaper's political writers. On Wednesday, January 26, Butchko's announcement of candidacy was published in the Valley View along with his picture. However, Butchko and Brian could not ascertain that his announcement of the candidacy had been published in the other major newspapers in the District. Corey's announcement had apparently not been published in any other paper besides the Valley Publications. But Butchko's campaign now had received substantial publicity, and it had a lot of momentum. It would take some doing for any candidate to defeat him.

On Tuesday, January 25, Nixon had announced in a nationwide TV broadcast that he had presented a secret eight point secret offer to the North Vietnamese on October 11 of 1971, which included 1. A total withdrawal of all united states military forces from South Vietnam within six months of an agreement; 2. Free and democratic elections in South Vietnam within six months of an agreement; and six other points.

Butchko thought that the requirement of free and democratic elections was probably unworkable since it did not seem that free elections were an established part of the way of life in Vietnamese civilization. Yet, the proposal of free and democratic elections sounded good. Therefore Butchko planned to point out in his subsequent speeches that Vietnamese civilization was a separate civilization with its own way of life, its own institutions, and patterns of government, and that it was unrealistic to insist on the establishment of free elections or any particular form of government in South Vietnam as a condition of our final withdrawal.

On Friday, February 4, Butchko appeared at a meeting of the North East Valley Democratic Club at the Pacoima Congregational Church in Pacoima. Tom Bradley spoke at that meeting. Corey and his campaign manager, Kenneth Goyer, were there. Mr. Goyer said that he had hoped to dissuade Butchko from running, but that he had seen Butchko's snipe signs and so he expected that Butchko would indeed file. Corey put some of his one-page photocopied literature on the windshields of the parked cars of those in attendance. Following the meeting, Butchko attended an exciting cocktail party at the home of one of the club members. Tom Bradley and Nate Holden were also at the party, and they exchanged greetings with Butchko.

Butchko continued to snipe almost every night until the primary election. He realized that it was important to keep his signs up all times, and when other candidates began to snipe it was, of course necessary to attend to sniping every week. Butchko enjoyed sniping because it gave him an opportunity for some privacy.

On Tuesday, February 8, Butchko attended a meeting of the County Committee. Les Rivers said to Butchko that it was good to see him. After the meeting, Butchko met with Brian, and they completed the work on his campaign brochure. Brian arranged to have the brochure printed so that it would be available in time for the McGovern caucus on Saturday, February 12. Butchko had written the text of the brochure with Brian's

162

assistance, and some contributions from Ted Lane, who was then the chairman of the Twenty-Seventh Congressional Democratic Council. The brochure had Butchko's positions on the major issues. It called for setting a definite date for prompt and complete disengagement of all our military forces from Vietnam and Indochina. It stated that Butchko favored amnesty in connection with the Vietnam War. A contribution from Ted Lane stated that Butchko favored extending social security benefits available to persons who reach 60 years of age. The front cover of the brochure included Butchko's picture, and the words "Peace, Progress, Jobs," in large capital letters, along with his name and the office and the slogan, "It's time for a change." Throughout the campaign, Butchko would hear many favorable comments on his brochure. Ben Polin, a long-time activist in the Sunland-Tujunga Democratic Club, said it was the best political brochure he had ever seen.

On Saturday, February 12, Butchko appeared at the McGovern delegate selection caucus for the Twenty-Seventh Congressional District at Taft High School. He made his brochures available at the caucus. He did not seek to be elected as a delegate because he truly felt that the honors should be distributed as widely as possible, and he was content to be Congressional candidate supporting McGovern.

On Monday, February 14, Butchko took out filing papers at the offices of the Los Angeles County Registrar of Voters. He saw Corey there.

On Wednesday, February 16, the Valley View published an article stating that Butchko would address the Reseda-West Valley Democrat Club at the Lane's home in Canoga Park that evening. Butchko spoke at the meeting along with several other candidates. As planned, Butchko pointed out the reasons why we should not insist on

163

free elections in South Vietnam as a condition of withdrawal. Ted Lane told Butchko that he had made a very good speech. Corey arrived after Butchko spoke, and he was afforded an opportunity to speak but he declined.

On Friday, February 18, Butchko attended a banquet honoring Tom Carrell at the Sportsman's Lodge in Studio City. Tom and Butchko exchanged greetings. There was a very good attendance at this banquet. Jess Unruh, Sigmund Arywitz and, the State Chairman of the AFL-CIO, were there. Local Democratic office-holders were there. Corman was there, and Corman attacked Nixon in a major speech. Butchko met Harold Keith, a wealthy Democrat from Malibu who told Butchko that he would probably run for Congress in the Twenty-Seventh District. Portions of Malibu were in the new Twenty-Seventh District. Butchko exchanged greetings with many people at this banquet and told them that he was running for Congress in the Twenty-Seventh District.

On January 26, it was stated in the Times that Les Cleveland, the mayor of Simi, was considering running for Congress in the Twenty-Seventh Congressional District. Brian learned that Cleveland was a former Methodist minister and that he had been Corman's minister. Simi was not in the district; however, and eventually Cleveland decided to run for Congress in the other district in Ventura County where he was unopposed for the Democratic nomination.

On Saturday, February 19, Butchko attended an issues conference sponsored by the Democratic State Central Committee at the Los Angeles Convention Center. Butchko and Ed Burke, a social studies teacher at Chatsworth High School, met and discussed the elections at this conference. Burke said that he was considering running for the Democratic nomination for State Senator in the Twenty-Third State Senate District. This

164

would put him contention with Joe McGhee. Burke said he had been asked to run by Fred Ball.

At this time, Butchko's information was to the effect that Fred Ball was supporting Corey against Butchko.

On Tuesday, February 22, Butchko attended a McGovern petition party at Jay Moss' home in Northridge. He made his brochures available at this party. Brian also attended a petition party and obtained the rest of 40 signatures that Butchko needed to file for the Congressional election. On February 23, Butchko returned his filing papers to the offices of the Registrar of Voters. Butchko thus became the first candidate to officially file for the Democratic nomination for Congress in the Twenty-Seventh Congressional District in 1972.

On February 25, Butchko had picked up campaign quarter cards and quarter sheets which he had previously ordered at Majestic Poster Press in Los Angeles. He soon began to snipe with these, using them on telephone poles and other places that were suitable for sniping. Corey began sniping in February using quarter sheets that were less colorful and less attractive than Butchko's. But Corey also did a lot of sniping, and at some times especially during the early part of the campaign, he was competitive with Butchko in the sniping arena.

On Friday, February 25, Butchko attended a meeting of the Sunland-Tujunga Democratic Club at Nancy Lund's house in Sunland. He made his brochures available at this meeting, and he exchanged greetings with Luther Mandel, who was running for the Democratic nomination for Congress in the new Twenty-Sixth Congressional District, which included portions of Burbank and the entire northern portion of Los Angeles

165

County. At this meeting, the Club elected its delegates to the forthcoming California Democratic Council Convention. Butchko was nominated. When he spoke on his behalf, he reminded the club members that he was a peace candidate and their candidate for Congress in 1968,

Butchko was easily elected as a delegate since the number of candidates for delegates was exactly equal to the Club's quota of delegates. Butchko regarded his election as a delegate at this meeting as a victory of sorts.

On Sunday, February 26, Butchko received major publicity in the Valley News and Green Sheet for his forthcoming appearance and speech at the February 28 meeting of the Twenty-Seventh California Democratic Council, which was now expanding into the San Fernando Valley Democratic Council. The meeting was held at the Pacoima Congregational Church in Pacoima. In this speech, Butchko said that in 1968, the California Democratic Council had contributed mightily to the movement that induced Johnson to halt the bombing of North Vietnam and to go to the conference table at Paris, and that now it had an opportunity to follow through on this important political work. Butchko attacked Nixon's Vietnam War policies as he did in all his 1972 speeches.

On February 29, Butchko drove to Oxnard and Port Hueneme and began sniping there. He noticed that Corey had already done some sniping there. Butchko kept his signs up in Oxnard and Port Hueneme throughout most of the campaign.

On Thursday, March 2, the Los Feliz Hills News published an article stating that Butchko was the first candidate to officially file in the Twenty-Seventh Congressional District and giving his background.

On Saturday, March 4, Butchko attended the opening of the Duberchin for Assembly Headquarters in Sherman Oaks. Butchko exchanged greetings with Harold Keith and his campaign manager, Gary Mussel. Gary said Harold would probably run. Butchko there signed Joe McGhee's filing papers. Joe said that the race in the Twenty-Seventh then seemed to be between Butchko and Corey, and that Butchko was ahead. Joe said that Joe Ball was now supporting Harold Keith against Butchko. The members of a Young Democrats Club were also in attendance at this event as they were at many others in that campaign. Some of them indicated that they were supporting Harold Keith at that time. Butchko spoke with a Catholic college girl who said that she stopped working for Van de Kamp in 1969 when she learned that he had prosecuted Doctor Spock.

On March 7, 1972, Butchko attended a meeting of the McGovern Speakers Bureau in Beverly Hills. Also March 7, McGovern made a surprisingly strong showing in the New Hampshire primary although Muskie won that primary.

On Friday, March 10, Butchko spoke at a candidate's night program at the home of Jay Moss in Northridge. Several days earlier, Butchko had learned that Mark Novak an attorney in Beverly Hills, who lived in Encino, had filed for the Democratic nomination in the Twenty-Seventh Congressional District. Novak was virtually unknown in politics, Butchko had never even heard of Novak before 1972. None of Butchko's friends had heard of Novak before 1972. However, Novak had won in the balloting for delegates in the Twenty-Seventh Congressional District. In the McGovern delegate selection caucus Novak along with several other men were dropped from the delegate list because of the quota limiting the number of male delegates. Only Art Carstens had been retained as a male McGovern delegate in the Twenty-Seventh.

At this meeting, which took place on the last day of filing for office, Butchko was surprised to learn that several additional candidates had filed. Bob McIhnerny, an insurance broker, who lived in Pasadena, had filed in the Twenty-Seventh. James Blaine Jennings, an attorney who lived in Malibu, had filed. Mark Mitchell an attorney filed. Harold Keith had not filed.

At this meeting, Corey spoke first among the candidates in the Twenty-Seventh. He spoke briefly, and Butchko's sense of fairness led him to speak briefly also. He said that he had been a peace candidate in 1968, and again attacked Nixon. Novak spoke next and took about twice as much time as Corey and Butchko combined. McIhnerny also spoke, and he did not seem impressive to Butchko on this occasion or on any other occasion during the campaign.

After the speeches, a labor official from the East told Butchko that he liked Butchko's talk the most, and that it had punch. Butchko now concluded that he would have tough opposition in the primary for several reasons. The large number of candidates (6) would tend to lessen the impact of any one campaign and make it more difficult to get publicity. Novak's name was sufficiently similar to Butchko's from an ethnic point of view to cause some confusion, and to take some ethnic votes from Butchko. Novak was a fair speaker, although Butchko thought that he was a better speaker than Novak.

On March 14, Butchko attended the meeting of the Los Angeles County Democratic Central Committee.

On March 15, Butchko was interviewed by the Twenty-Seventh District Interviewing Committee of the Set the Date Campaign. The Set the Date Campaign was a new and loosely organized peace group, which was now working on endorsements of candidates. The local interviewing committee included Kathleen Sexton, Jerry Raskin, Louis Webb, a Blackman, Bob Feinstein, the President of a non- California Democratic Council Democratic Club in the West Valley, and a lesser known woman. Butchko handled this interview very well, and answered many of the foreign policy questions in an original and scholarly manner. Butchko distributed his brochures among the members of the interviewing committee. He was the only candidate who had printed literature at this time. Novak was also interviewed that evening.

Several days later, Brian told Butchko that Louis Webb had been very favorably impressed by Butchko's performance before the Interviewing Committee, and that Novak had been unimpressive in his interview. Butchko now thought he had a chance to get that endorsement.

Also on March 15, the Valley View published a Butchko press release wherein it was stated that Butchko was the first candidate to file for the Democratic nomination in the Twenty-Seventh District. The article also gave Butchko's background.

On March 14 or 16, Butchko and Brian went to Gangi Studios in North Hollywood and ordered 25 sheets for use on small billboards maintained by Kennedy Outdoor Advertising Company. These were less expensive than the larger billboards, and they were almost as effective. They included the statements: Elect John T. Butchko to Congress in gold letters, and Peace, Progress, Jobs in smaller white letters at the bottom, all on a blue background.

On the weekend of March 17, 18, and 19, Butchko attended the California Democratic Council Convention in Oakland as a delegate representing the Sunland-Tujunga Democratic Club. At the dinner and caucus of delegates from the San Fernando Valley, Butchko made a good speech. He said that Nixon was attempting to prolong the war in Vietnam in a vain and futile effort to save face: that Nixon was attempting to postpone the inevitable day when it had to be admitted that the entire war policy was tragic mistake. He attacked Goldwater, Jr., for the views which he had expressed about the war. In 1970, Goldwater had enthusiastically supported the Nixon invasion of Cambodia. Butchko pointed out that he had been a peace candidate and had won a nomination for Congress in a District situated in the San Fernando Valley. He attacked Nixon and Goldwater, Jr., for policies of repression. He would use these themes in many subsequent speeches. Butchko urged support for uncompromising peace candidates, and he called for endorsement of McGovern. He also pointed out his earlier active support of peace candidates dating back to 1966.

Novak was not a delegate to the Convention, and he was still not a member of a California Democratic Council Club. But Novak, assisted by a law partner, appeared and spoke at the caucus. Novak was clearly less impressive than Butchko. Novak now brought with him some mimeographed campaign literature. During the Convention, Butchko learned that Novak was Jewish. In this and subsequent literature, Novak would firmly call for military support for Israel. At the caucus, Ted Lane inquired of Nancy Lund what she had done to make arrangements for the local endorsing convention. Her answer indicated that she had not yet done anything.

170

Although McGovern did not get the 60% vote required for endorsement by the CDC, McGovern did get the support of the CDC. Butchko thought McGovern probably would have got the required 60% vote for endorsement, if McGovern could have attended and spoke to the Convention. McGovern did get the support of the California Democratic Council; that required only a 51% vote. Richard Bergholz, the political editor of the Los Angeles Times, wrote that the California Democratic Council had voted to support McGovern.

Toni Kimmell had written an article for the Statewide California Democratic Council publication calling for no endorsement of McGovern or any presidential candidate. Of course, McGovern was the only candidate who had a chance for the endorsement, and his vote was over 50%. During the time of the Convention, Vance Hartke withdrew from the Presidential race. But Shirley Chisholm was still a candidate, and a substantial number of delegates were supporting her. There were also a number of other Democratic candidates still in the race for the Presidential nomination, including Muskie and Humphrey. As things turned out, McGovern did not need the endorsement of the California Democratic Council to win the California primary, but the support of the California Democratic Council was helpful to McGovern.

Brian drove Butchko back to Burbank after the Convention. Butchko knew that Brian's car was bugged, but anyway, he discussed some important matters on this return trip. Butchko pointed out that Novak's literature stated that; "We (should) withdraw all troops and logistical support and cease bombing as soon as it is possible to do so without jeopardy to American personnel. We should agree to elections under international supervision to create a freely elected government in Saigon, and we should negotiate for

171

the release of American prisoners concurrent with the withdrawal of our troops and the establishment of the election process." Butchko carefully pointed out the deficiencies in Novak's position statement by reason of which the statement did not go nearly far enough for a sound peace candidate in 1972. Butchko said that if we to wait for free elections before withdrawing troops, we might have to wait for a hundred years. Butchko said he intended to criticize this position statement of Novaks. Brian said that he had heard Novak say that Novak was going to run a relatively conservative campaign. Shortly after his return from the convention Butchko attended a party for Mc Govern supporters in Van Nuys. Novak was also there. Kathleen Sexton approached Butchko, and told him that there was a lot of interest in him on the Set the Date Committee. Butchko told her that in his opinion, the candidate they had endorsed did not meet the Committee's standards. Butchko had already ordered the space and sheets for his Kennedy Boards, and it was too late for any other candidate to order space for such boards

On Monday, April 3, Butchko and Novak both spoke briefly at a meeting of the San Fernando Valley Democratic Council in Studio City. Butchko assured the delegates to the Council that if nominated, he would put on one of the biggest campaigns for Congress that they had ever seen in the San Fernando Valley. Novak showed up in work clothes, and he said it was because he had just been involved in Little League Baseball with his son.

At this meeting, Toni Kimmell could be seen giving some encouragement to Novak. At this meeting, Novak told Butchko that Clyde Bullock had told him that Bob McIhnerny had got the COPE endorsement. He said that Mr. Bullock said that the reasons why COPE endorsed McIhnerny were that he had stepped aside in 1969 to allow

172

John Van de Kamp to run in the special election in the Twenty-Seventh Congressional District, and that COPE liked McIhnerny a lot for having done that. Butchko had also heard that McIhnerny had some friends in COPE. Brian was pleased that Novak had not got the COPE endorsement. But it subsequently turned out that this endorsement meant that McIhnerny would have a big campaign in May, and thus Butchko would be competing against two big campaigns, in addition to the lesser ones.

On Wednesday, April 5, Butchko was the only candidate to appear at the meeting of the Reseda-West Valley Club at the home of Ted and Ida Lane in Canoga Park. Butchko spoke for a few minutes, attacking Nixon and Goldwater, Jr. Butchko said that the Club could demonstrate that it was the most effective political force in the West Valley by working to elect Butchko to congress.

On April 6, Butchko was interviewed by the interviewing committee of Women For at their office in Beverly Hills. Butchko was told that the interviewing committee was very busy since there were so many candidates and that they wanted to handle his interview somewhat rapidly. Butchko obliged by distributing his brochure. He said that it contained his basic positions on the major issues, and also a summary of his background. He said that in 1968, he had been a peace candidate and he had won the Democratic nomination for congress in the Twenty-Seventh Congressional District. During the questioning, he was asked for his views on aid to Israel, including selling Phantom Jets to Israel. Butchko indicated that it was important to prevent another war in the Middle East, and that requests for aid would have to be considered and decided according to the particular situation at the time, and that he would be willing to supply such aid as might be needed to ensure the survival of Israel. Butchko expected that

Novak would take a more hawkish position on this question and he knew that a high percentage of the Women For group were Jewish, but Butchko did not like to compromise on important issues. At that time, Israel held all of the "conquered territories" or "occupied lands".

Butchko was asked about the expenditures he would make in his primary campaign. He answered fully and truthfully pointing out that he had ordered boards and that his boards would soon be up; and he would have much newspaper advertising, and that he could and would do all this with his own money. At this time, Butchko was still the only candidate with printed literature, the only candidate besides Corey who had sniped, and the candidate who had got the most publicity. Brian assured him that it was too late for the other candidates to obtain billboard space, and that Butchko would be the only candidate to have boards.

When asked about other endorsements, Butchko had to say that another candidate had the COPE endorsement, and that still another candidate had been endorsed by the Set the Date Committee. This was certain to be a serious drawback to Butchko's chances for endorsement by Women For. So Butchko pointed out that in Novak's mimeographed literature, Novak had called for withdrawal concurrent with the establishment of free elections, and that if we had to wait for free elections in South Vietnam, we might have to wait for a hundred years.

On April 7, Brian arranged to have Butchko's literature and bumper stickers available at the candidate's forum at Cleveland High School in Reseda. On April 7, Butchko attended an opening of the McGovern headquarters in Van Nuys. He exchanged greetings with Art Carstens and Dennis Weaver, an actor who was now active in the

174

McGovern campaign, and he made some additional acquaintances. Art Carstens told Butchko that he saw Butchko's signs all over the Valley. At this time, Ida Lane was working in that headquarters. Ted Lane would later be active in the McGovern Headquarters in Reseda. They had been supporting McGovern in 1971.

Also on April 7 the Los Angeles Times, San Fernando Valley edition, published a little article stating that Mark Novak, "Democratic candidate for Congress, in the Twenty-Seventh congressional District", would open his West Valley headquarters on Ventura Boulevard in Tarzana that evening." This was a large headquarters in a good location on Ventura Boulevard near Reseda Boulevard. In May, Bob McIhnerny would open a headquarters across the street from Novak's. So April 7 was about the time that Novak's campaign started to reach the public. On April 8, ten of Butchko's boards went up in the West Valley. Several weeks later in the month, an additional five of his boards would go up, and early in May an additional five of his boards would go up making a total of twenty boards in the West Valley, not counting the three boards on Butchko's headquarters.

In May, Joe McGhee was so impressed by Butchko's boards that he asked Butchko how many boards Butchko had. There were also 3 of Butchko's boards on his headquarters.

On Sunday, April 9, Butchko spoke at a meeting of Bob Feinstein's Club in the West Valley. Also, as a part of the discussion of issues, he took on the busing issue, which Nixon was emphasizing. He pointed out that the federal courts had ordered busing only where necessary to overcome the effect of the drawing of boundaries of certain school districts in a way that could be said to foster segregation, and that the federal

175

courts had not ordered busing to achieve racial balance as stated by Nixon. Butchko pointed out that there had been more bussing for segregation in the past then for integration now.

One of the members of the Young Democrats Club was at this meeting, and he told Butchko that he had seen some of his boards and that they were very attractive. But as Butchko went to and came from the meeting, he saw Novak's quarter cards on telephone poles in the far western portion of the West Valley. Novak was reaching an increasing number of the public. Nixon then resumed the bombing of North Vietnam since is seemed that Butchko's potential of becoming a two-time nominee for Congress was slipping away. On April 5, Butchko began his newspaper advertising campaign with an ad in the Valley View. All the ads would be the same as this one. They included his picture and the statements "Vote For Peace-Progress-Jobs. Elect John T. Butchko to Congress. 'A man you can trust.'"

In 1972 Butchko made all the difference. The main reason why Nixon did not renew the bombing of Vietnam before this time was Butchko's political potential.

Beginning in the last week in April, Butchko would have heavy advertising with this ad in the Valley View every week until the end of the campaign, in the Green Sheet first on Tuesdays and Sundays to include the Thursday and Friday editions toward the end of the campaign. In May he had the ad inserted in the Thursday and Sunday editions of the San Fernando Valley Sections of the Times, and to include the Friday edition toward the end of the campaign. In May, he had the ad inserted every week in the Press Courier in Oxnard and Port Hueneme and in the Malibu Times in Malibu. In the last two weeks before the election, he ran the ad in the Valley Publications.

176

Throughout his campaign, Butchko did a tremendous amount of work, preparing press releases and mailing them to all the newspapers in the district, and to some nearby newspapers, which may have taken some interest in the district. There were about twenty such releases. Some of them related to events. Some described the contents of his very recent speeches, and some were statements of his issues positions, and some were attacks on Goldwater, Jr.

During the primary campaign Butchko fed into the surveillance network books critical of U.S. involvement in the war in Vietnam. This helped McGovern.

On Wednesday, April 12, Butchko spoke at a meeting of the United Valley Democratic Club in Woodland Hills. This was a non-CDC Club, and Butchko satisfactorily covered all of the major issues. When asked about constructive goals for the country, he said that we should work on spreading peace throughout the world. McIhnerny and Jennings also spoke at this meeting. Novak had spoken at an earlier meeting of the club.

Butchko could sense that Novak's campaign had picked up a lot of momentum, and that Butchko would have a struggle on his hands just to get the California Democratic Council endorsement.

On April 13, Butchko spoke at a crowded candidates' night program sponsored by the San Fernando Valley Democratic Association at the United Auto Workers Hall in Van Nuys. The candidates were told they could have five minutes. Butchko was asked to speak first. He spoke for four minutes and answered questions for one minute. He had a lot more to say since his notes now contained a speech of about ten to fifteen minutes covering all the major issues. But Butchko had covered the issues of the war,

177

unemployment and inflation, amnesty and the draft, together with attacks on Nixon and Goldwater, Jr.

McIhnerny and Jennings also spoke. But Novak spoke for about fifteen minutes. Butchko was, of course, displeased to Novak take so much time in violation of the rules. But Novak made one of his flashier presentations; and having taken so much time, Novak had an opportunity to make a favorable impression on this occasion. Most observers do not seem to be bothered by a speaker who takes a lot more time than his competitors all in violation of the rules. A lot of candidates for other offices in the Valley had been there, and Butchko knew that Novak had gained ground, and that Butchko would have an uphill struggle to get the California Democratic Council endorsement.

On the morning of Monday, April 17, Butchko and Novak both spoke to four successive social studies classes at Agoura High School in Agoura. The candidates each spoke for about 20 minutes to each class and shared the rest of the time answering questions. The teacher who was presiding over these speeches said that he could probably vote for Butchko. Novak now had a printed brochure. It was first class, but Butchko thought that his own brochure was better. It was 50% longer. In these talks, Butchko hit hard at Nixon's recent resumption of the widespread bombing of North Vietnam. Butchko outlined the history of the war in Vietnam, and the contributions of the peace movement in bringing pressure to bear on the national administrations, first to halt the bombing of North Vietnam for over three years, to go to the peace table at Paris, and to withdraw most of our ground forces from South Vietnam. Butchko now began to use a brief statement calling for ethics in government and for electing leaders with the courage to take advanced positions on the issues and with better ethical standards and a

178

sense of moral purpose, rather than persons such as Nixon who were primarily concerned with perpetuating themselves in office and who were therefore willing to perpetuate their worst mistakes in their efforts to stay in office. Butchko and Novak were not yet attacking each other in speeches.

On Tuesday, April 18, Butchko, Novak, McIhnerny and Jennings spoke at the candidate's night program sponsored by the Las Virgenes Valley League of Women Voters in Agoura High School. Butchko spoke satisfactorily covering the major issues and handling the questions satisfactorily. In all his speeches now, Butchko was pointing out that he had been a peace candidate who had won the Democratic nomination for Congress in the former Twenty-Seventh Congressional District situated predominantly in the San Fernando Valley. Novak said that he was not a latecomer to the peace movement, and that he had been a co-founder of the Westside Committee of Concern, a peace group in 1965. Butchko had never heard of that group, and none of Butchko's friends had ever heard of Novak before 1972. But Novak was now trying hard to prevent Butchko from using Butchko's heavy, consistent and early involvement in the peace movement to advantage over Novak. McIhnerny spoke very unimpressively on this occasion. He said he would be patronizing the audience if he talked about unemployment, or about inflation.

On Wednesday, April 19, Butchko, Novak, Corey and Jennings spoke at the crowded Reseda-West Valley Club Candidates Night Program at Grover Cleveland High School in Reseda. Corey told Butchko that the California Democratic Council endorsement now seemed to be a toss up between Butchko and Novak. Butchko thought that this was the way it looked to Corey, but that Novak was probably ahead in the race for that endorsement. Corey did not like Novak. Butchko arranged to speak last among the candidates in the Twenty-Seventh.

The candidates each had about 15 minutes to speak and some additional time for questions. Louis Webb had put Butchko's brochures on all the seats in the auditorium. Novak said something about breaking up some big corporate conglomerates in his speech, and he said he could say that without waiting to hear another candidate talk first. Novak may have had in mind the preceding night's talks in Agoura where Butchko got Novak to answer questions before Butchko answered them. Butchko was right in trying to get Novak to go first because Novak had been breaking the rules and taking too much time. Unless the rules were strictly enforced, this tactic could only be overcome if Novak spoke first.

In his own speech, Butchko said that unlike the preceding candidate (Novak), Butchko had not had to change his campaign literature, and he pointed out the position on Vietnam that Novak had taken in his original literature, why it was deficient, and he said he was glad that in Novak's more recent literature, his position on this issue had been changed to correspond with Butchko's. After Butchko's speech, Novak told him that the campaign had been escalated tonight. Brian said that Novak had been upset by Butchko's criticism.

On Friday, April 21, Butchko attended the opening of the McGovern Headquarters in Reseda. Butchko was introduced as a peace candidate by Mike Goldberg, the acting president of the Sherman Oaks Democratic Club and a figure in the recently organized Valley Citizens for McGovern Committee, which was running the various Valley McGovern Headquarters. There was also a McGovern Headquarters in

Encino. Novak arrived after Butchko had left and spoke when introduced by Goldberg. Ted Lane complained to and criticized Goldberg for allowing Novak to speak. Before Butchko was introduced, he had been told by a program coordinator that candidates would be introduced but that they should not make speeches.

The endorsing conventions were held at Valley City College in North Hollywood on the afternoon of Sunday, April 23. Novak supporter now wore Novak buttons. Members of the Young Democrats Club were in attendance, and they were a solid bloc of votes for Novak. Ted Lane had some questions about whether they were qualified delegates to the convention, but he let them vote.

Ted and Ida Lane, Rita Strickland and her husband, Dick Fitzgerald, Brian, Joe McGhee and several other persons were known to be favorable to Butchko. Travers was complaining that Mike Goldberg had not notified the delegates of the Sherman Oaks Club about the convention, and that they had not come. Travers said Goldberg told him that he thought it wasn't important.

Arline Mathews and her husband, Ray Mathews, were leading support for Novak, who would soon be paying them for press releases. They were also active in the Valley Citizens for McGovern. Ed Burke was there and would vote for Novak. Arline Mathews, at Novak's request, made an attempt to have Butchko disqualified from being a delegate. This attempt was voted down. McIhnerny and Corey also sought the endorsement, and a sixty percent vote was required.

The candidates each spoke for five minutes and had some additional time to answer questions. Butchko made a good hard hitting speech. He mentioned that some of the delegates had worked together with him in 1967 and 1968 to place on the California

Primary ballot a slate of delegates opposed to the re-nomination of Lyndon Johnson, and that by so doing they had helped to initiate a series of events which put a halt to the bombing of North Vietnam, and that all this led to the increased pressure for troop withdrawals. Butchko again criticized the deficiencies in the position on Vietnam in Novak's original campaign literature, while pointing out that Novak had changed it to correspond to Butchko's position. Butchko seemed to be by far the stronger speaker on this occasion. He had been nominated by Brian and seconded by Rita Stricklin. Novak had been nominated by Arline Mathews. A 60% vote was needed for endorsement. Novak got it with about 28 votes to about 11 for Butchko.

Soon after the Convention, it was learned that the Young Democrats were sniping for Novak. Whether he was paying them was not known. Their sniping never came close to matching Butchko's. Soon after this convention, Irv Ruven, the California Democratic Council endorsed candidate for Assembly said he saw Butchko campaign signs every ten feet. This was to some extent an exaggeration.

After this convention, Novak was the front runner, although Butchko had put on a better campaign to that time. Butchko was now sure that he would not get any significant endorsements regardless of what might happen during the remainder of the campaign.

On April 27, Butchko, Novak and McIhnerny spoke at a Democratic candidate's night program at the civic auditorium in Oxnard. The program was taped and televised locally in Oxnard and Port Hueneme. The candidates made their full speeches. Butchko said that the Nixon Administration stood for retaliation in addition to repression. The candidates fielded questions on all kinds of issues. But Novak left before the question period was completed. He said he had to attend a meeting in Malibu. The local

182

Democrats, including Ed Albrecht, the president of the Oxnard Democratic Club, told Butchko that he had come over very well on television. Brian was soon told that the local Democrats thought Butchko did better than Novak on this occasion, and that he came over better on television. He was also told that some of the local Democrats did not trust Novak. After the primary, Joe Flynn, who had been elected Supervisor, in Ventura County, told Brian that Butchko had done better than Novak on this program.

On Friday, April 28, Butchko opened his headquarters in an excellent location on Sherman Way near Topanga Canyon Blvd., in Canoga Park. The opening included a party that evening. It was attended by Butchko, Brian, Louis Webb and some of his friends, Ted Lane, the Stricklins, and Ed Guyot. Butchko had got publicity for the headquarters opening in the Valley View, the Valley Green Sheet and the Los Angeles Times, San Fernando Valley edition.

On Saturday, April 29, Butchko did some sniping in Malibu. He had done some sniping there during the first week in April. But a highway patrol officer saw Butchko sniping. He stopped Butchko and made him take down the signs he had put up on telephone poles. Corey and Jenning's signs were left up in Malibu. Butchko was convinced that sniping on telephone poles and bus benches without advertising should never be interfered with by public authorities. Sniping was an important part of the election process, which enabled non-wealthy candidates to compete for public office. On May 2, Butchko attended a meeting of the Los Angeles County Democratic Central Committee. Les Rivers asked the candidates present to stand and to be introduced. Butchko was thus introduced as a candidate. At a joint appearance of Butchko and

Novak in the West Valley in May, someone said to Novak, "How are you doing?" Or "Who is winning?" Novak answered, "He (indicating Butchko) has the boards."

In late April or early May, Corey sent to Butchko a sample of a photocopied letter that Novak and some of his supporters were using. The salutation of the letter said "Dear fellow McGovern supporter." The letter said that "Although there are other worthy candidates for the nomination, we believe, after careful consideration of them all, that Mark Novak represents our best hope of defeating Goldwater. The letter asked for campaign contributions. It was signed by Kathleen Sexton designated as "McGovern Delegate," Stanley Charnofsky, "Professors for McGovern", Phil Friedman, "Teachers for McGovern", Steve Koff "SFVSC Students for McGovern", Art Carstens, "McGovern Delegate," Richard P. Haddon, "Coordinator Valley United Ministry," and Arthur D. Sorosky M.D., "Doctors for McGovern". Corey apparently felt this was unfair to Butchko since he had observed Butchko's support for McGovern in 1971 when Novak had been unheard of in politics.

But the letter was a minor matter compared to what was uncovered next. On about May 3 or 4, Brian learned from Luke Perry, a campaign worker for Joe McGhee, that the precinct walkers for the McGovern Headquarters in Van Nuys (and Reseda) had been carrying and distributing Novak's brochure along with their McGovern literature. The McGovern Headquarters in Encino was also run by the Valley Citizens for McGovern Committee, and Brian thought that the McGovern Headquarters in Encino also had precinct walkers carry and distribute Novak literature. Brian and Louis Webb conferred with Kathleen Sexton at the McGovern Headquarters in Van Nuys. She told him that precinct walkers for McGovern had not been required to carry Novak's

184

materials, but that some may have done it voluntarily. Brian went to the headquarters in Van Nuys and was outraged to see large quantities of Novak's brochures stacked in the room where the McGovern precinct walker's kits were filled. Many of the kit fillers and precinct walkers were youths who did not know about the struggle going on between Butchko and Novak. Butchko instructed Brian to call the main McGovern Campaign offices in Washington, D.C. and in Los Angeles for the purpose of having the McGovern campaign chiefs stop the Valley McGovern Headquarters from distributing Novak's materials in their precinct operations. Brian did so. Miles Rubin, a chief of the Southern California campaign, told Brian that McGovern was not endorsing local candidates and that it was improper for McGovern Headquarters to distribute materials for a local candidate in its precinct operations. Mr. Rubin told Brian that he would investigate the situation, and that if this had been done in the Valley Headquarters, he would stop it. It was stopped. Brian then took into the McGovern Headquarters photocopies of the letters, which McGovern had sent to Butchko in 1971 thanking Butchko for his early support. Of course, the leaders of the Valley Citizens for McGovern Committee all knew that Butchko was supporting McGovern and had done so consistently.

On May 10, Butchko and Novak showed up for speeches at El Camino High School in the far western portion of the West Valley. However, the students decided to have the speech outside, so as to get a larger audience. But once outside, they could not find the microphone during the recreational period, and so the speeches were never made.

Since Novak had been prevented from using the McGovern precinct operation in the Valley to carry his literature, he would have to get some money to ensure his victory in the primary. The money was forthcoming from groups such as Women For, which

185

endorsed Novak in May. Californians for Liberal Representation, of which Art Carstens was the Chairman, also endorsed Novak. Butchko he informed Californians for Liberal Representation earlier in the year that he would like to ask for their endorsement and to interviewed as required. But Californians for Liberal Representation did not conduct interviews in the Twenty-Seventh Congressional District.

On May 12, Butchko attended a peace rally sponsored by the Valley Peace Center at Reseda Park in Reseda. Pat Arnold, the chairwoman of the Peace Center, was in charge. Pat Arnold was supporting Novak. Novak was there and sure to speak. Butchko kept asking Pat Arnold for a chance to speak, and she kept putting him off. Novak spoke early in the program. He was introduced as "the Democratic candidate for Congress in the Twenty-Seventh Congressional District." Eventually Pat Arnold told Butchko that there wouldn't be any time for his speech. But he said he would only take five minutes, and that he insisted on it in the interests of fairness. So he was allowed to speak at the end of the program immediately after the emcee had encouraged the audience to join a peace march then starting on Reseda Boulevard. Butchko was introduced as "John Butchko of the John Butchko office." There were still some people in attendance, and Butchko made a strong hard-hitting speech as he had done before when speaking outside. While the audience had been at its peak, Louis Webb had distributed Butchko's brochures, and put Butchko's snipe sheets on trees in the park.

In the second week in May, McIhnerny began his sniping operations. He had hired a professional sniper from northern California, and he had a tremendous amount of sniping done before the primary election.

In April, Butchko learned that he had not been invited to participate in and speak at the San Fernando Valley State College Political Forum of 1972. Novak had spoken there. In 1968, Butchko had been officially invited to participate in the Forum, and he had had a booth and had made a good speech there. He had also spoken at a Valley State College political program late in the general election campaign of 1968.

Unfortunately for Butchko, literature describing the Valley State Political Forum and listing the participants was widely circulated on the campus and at some other schools. This was very unfair to Butchko, and there was nothing he could do about it.

On May 13, Butchko attended a McGovern Party at the Unitarian Church on Sepulveda Boulevard in Northridge (or Granada Hills). Novak was also there. Butchko exchanged greetings with John Forsythe. Butchko stayed longer than Novak, met more people, and gave his brochures to more people.

On May 16, Butchko took to KPOL and KPSA some tapes of short speeches that he had made for broadcast on these radio stations in their free time for candidates programs.

In May through the June primary, Travers and his wife Leslie Chambers managed a California Democratic Council Headquarters in Sherman Oaks. When people called to ask whom to vote for in the Twenty-Seventh Congressional District, they said "John Butchko".

On May 17, Butchko attended the candidate's day program at Pierce College. Brian set up a table for his literature, and bumper stickers, and Butchko passed out his brochures to walkers-by. However, there were not enough people in the recreation hall to have an audience for a speech.

On the evening of May 17, Butchko spoke at a candidate's night program at a Jewish Temple in Northridge. Butchko made an excellent presentation discussing the history of the Vietnam War, the work of the peace movement, and the deceptive policies of the Nixon Administration. Novak, McIhnerny, and Mitchell also spoke. McIhnerny now had a brochure that included a picture of the former Democratic Governor, Pat Brown, who had endorsed McIhnerny. Someone in the audience said that the Democratic Party should be complimented on having so many fine candidates. Since Novak was now the front runner, statements such as this were now favorable to Butchko.

Jerry Brown, the son of the former Democratic Governor, had endorsed Muskie in 1971.

On May 18, Butchko spent the entire afternoon passing out his brochures in the vicinity of the Democratic booth at the Esplanade Shopping Center in Oxnard.

On Sunday, May 21, Butchko spent the afternoon passing out his brochures and talking to many people at a rally for McGovern at Devonshire Downs in Northridge. Butchko there exchanged greetings with Lloyd Bridges and gave him Butchko's brochure. A lady there said she heard that there were two attractive candidates in his race and he Butchko was one of them. Seymour Seid, President of a California Democratic Congressional Club in 1968, said to his son "Butchko is a good man."

On May 25, Butchko spoke on all the major issues to the Malibu Democratic Club in Malibu. They were impressed by Butchko.

In May, Butchko learned that Novak had also been endorsed by the United West Valley Democratic Club.

On May 31, Butchko and Novak spoke at the candidate's night program of the Valley Beth Shalom Temple in Encino. Novak now claimed that there had been nine endorsements by groups in this race, and that he had got eight of them. Butchko made a good speech covering the major issues.

On the afternoon of May 31, Butchko and Brian had learned that Novak had mailed his own campaign piece to every registered Democratic voter in the Twenty-Seventh District. Butchko had not known that Novak would get enough money to do this. Butchko then decided to do some heavy radio advertising in the San Fernando Valley. Brian made the necessary arrangements, and Butchko's radio advertising began on June 1 and continued until the morning of the primary on June 6. The radio ads said in part: "Democrats, Isn't it time we had a congressman. Elect John T. Butchko to Congress in the Twenty-Seventh District. Vote for Peace, Progress and Jobs. Elect John T. Butchko. He was right from the start. Don't be misled by paper endorsements representing a small fraction of 1% of the registered voters."

Novak then began his own heavy radio advertising on the night of May 31. Novak's ads referred to his endorsements, and included favorable comments by some of his endorsers.

Butchko also had radio advertising on the leading FM station in Ventura County.

On the morning of June 1, Butchko spoke and answered questions for about forty minutes to interested students at Birmingham High School in Van Nuys. In this speech as in many speeches since the California Democratic Council endorsing convention, Butchko said that the current disarmament negotiations (the SALT talks) should be broadened to include the Chinese. Butchko called for a Middle East Peace Conference to

189

include all the interested Middle East countries and also the United States and the Soviet Union. He also outlined the history of the war in Vietnam, the work of the peace movement, and the deceptive policies of the Nixon Administration. He pointed out that it was the bombing halt of 1968, which had led to the increased pressures for troop withdrawals.

Butchko said that the United States should use its influence with the Soviet Union to get Soviet troops out of Egypt.

On the evening of June 1, Butchko, Novak and McIhnerny spoke at a candidate's night program of the West Park Jewish Community Center at a junior high school in Canoga Park. Novak again claimed eight out of nine endorsements. Butchko said that he had not needed any endorsements to win the nomination in 1968, and that he would not need any to win in 1972. Butchko knew that it was important to continue to speak as a possible winner. In response to questions about the Middle East situation, Butchko said that the United States should take the lead in establishing a Middle East Peace Conference, and that a prompt settlement was in the best interests of Israel.

Someone in the audience said that all of these candidates are articulate.

On Saturday, June 3, Butchko manned his table at the candidates fair in the Esplanade Shopping Center in Oxnard. He got there in the morning, and he passed out his brochures to a lot of people throughout the day. The local Democrats told Butchko that he was campaigning effectively that day. Also on June 3, Brian and Louis Webb did some campaign work for Butchko at a political fair and Democratic Unity Rally in Santa Monica.

Novak also had a California Democratic Council slate mailer along with Ed Burke and the California Democratic Council endorsed candidate for Assembly in the Sixty-Fourth Assembly District. This mailer said that Novak had also been endorsed by Women For, the Set the Date Committee, and the United Valley Democratic Club. Novak ran a large ad in the Times and in the Valley Green Sheet on Sunday, June 4.

McIhnerny also mailed his own campaign piece to every registered Democrat in the district. This piece included a picture of Corman shaking hands with McIhnerny, and a picture of McIhnerny with Pat Brown. The mailer stated that McIhnerny was endorsed by Pat Brown. Of course, McIhnerny had got a lot of money and assistance from COPE. McIhnerny ran a large ad in the Times on Monday, June 5. In this ad, as in his mailer, it was said that McIhnerny was the one Democrat who could beat Goldwater.

On May 28, the Valley Green Sheet published an article in all editions wherein it was stated that Butchko had reaffirmed his support for George McGovern. The article also stated that Butchko had been praised by Senator McGovern for his efforts on behalf of the Democratic Party and that he had been praised by Hubert Humphrey for his contributions to the cause of peace.

On May 31, the Valley View published an article stating that Butchko had reaffirmed his support for McGovern.

Butchko along with the other candidates had his background and programs included in the candidate's pages of the Times, the Valley Green Sheet, the Las Virgenes Enterprise, and the Press-Courier (and perhaps the Thousand Oaks Chronicle). Butchko's name was first in alphabetical order, and for that reason he fared somewhat better than other candidates in the candidate's pages. In these statements, he called for

191

immediate withdrawal of all our military forces from Vietnam and Indochina. There were candidate's sections in the Valley Green Sheet and the Los Angeles Times.

Shortly before the 1972 primary, Ted Lane told Butchko that Novak was not a member of any California Democratic Council Club.

On Tuesday, June 6, Butchko joined Brian, Louis Webb and Rita Stricklin at his headquarters in Canoga Park. Because of difficulties in the vote counting operations, it was late at night before they got even some early returns. Butchko concluded from these that Novak would win the nomination.

The total votes were as follows: 1. Novak 25,835; 2. McIhnerny 13,725; 3. Butchko 8,306; 4. Mitchell 7,824; 5. Corey 7,478; 6. Jennings 6,548. Without the interference of Ed Davis, Butchko would have won the primary election on the strength of his boards. Ed Davis was the police chief of the City of Los Angeles.

Butchko concluded that Novak and McIhnerny's mailers had been their principal advantages. The money for these had largely come from some of the groups that had endorsed these two candidates.

The Novak campaign had got decisive assistance from some persons in surveillance, including members of the Los Angeles Police Department. Some of this assistance reached Novak indirectly. The surveillance persons of the Los Angeles Police Department led by Ed Davis were right-wingers and hawks. Ed Davis fed into this surveillance network matters to intimidate the Masons so that they would not vote for Butchko. Duane Baker, the Chief of Police of Glendale, also used improper surveillance activities against Butchko. Duane Baker was a right-winger and a hawk.

On Friday, June 9, Butchko received a telephone call from Novak. Novak started off by insulting Butchko. He then asked for Butchko's endorsement. Butchko told Novak that he endorsed him.

Novak's mailer late in the campaign would state that Novak had swept the Democratic Primary.

Butchko continued to attend meetings of the Los Angeles County Democratic Central Committee during the year. He attended numerous political meetings and parties, including the opening of the McGovern headquarters in Newhall and in Sunland.

At the opening of the McGovern Headquarters in Sunland, Butchko spoke with people there, including Bill Graham, a member of the Los Angeles County Democratic Central Committee.

McGovern won the California primary with 52% of the vote. It was a winner take all primary. Butchko had been instrumental in getting the nomination for McGovern. Defeating Butchko had taken so much out of some of the hawks that they could not stop McGovern. Butchko's support of McGovern also gave McGovern a big boost.

During the general election campaign, Butchko became the vice-chairman of the Unified Democratic Campaign Committee for the Sixty-Second Assembly District. Butchko received major publicity in the Valley Green Sheet in all editions for his endorsement of McGovern during the general election campaign. He also received major publicity in the Valley Green Sheet in all editions for his appearance at a California Democratic Council Conference in Santa Monica. There he spoke with people, including Travers Devine.

Shortly after Eagleton was dropped from the ticket, Butchko attended an important meeting of the McGovern's speakers Bureau in Los Angeles, where a prominent attorney, Malcolm Macky, said that Butchko might be appointed a judge because of his appellate briefs.

Butchko became active on the McGovern Speakers Bureau. As a member of the Speakers Bureau, he made three major speeches for McGovern: to the Newhall Optimists on September 12, to the East Hollywood Kiwanis Club on September 20, and to the Sears employees in Lancaster at 8:45 o'clock in the morning of October 19. Butchko was told that these were very good speeches.

Shortly after his speech for McGovern at the meeting of the Newhall Optimists, Butchko attended the grand opening of the Newhall McGovern Headquarters. There a young lady, Judy Dalton, said to the entire group that she had seen Butchko's speech to the Newhall Optimists and said Butchko was wonderful. Butchko exchanged greetings with Luther Mandel and/or his official campaign worker. Luther Mandel was the local candidate for Congress.

On the Saturday before McGovern dropped Eagleton from the ticket, Butchko attended a Democratic picnic in Crescenta Valley Park. Butchko spoke with people there. One lady said to some people that Butchko was a linguist. Ben Polin, a member of the Sunland-Tujunga Democratic Club and also a member of the Los Angeles County Democratic Central Committee, gave a speech describing Butchko's early and continuous support for McGovern, and said it was as though Butchko had a crystal ball. Butchko also exchanged greetings with the local candidate for State Senate, a Mr. Solomon.

194

In about September of 1972, Butchko attended an outdoors party of Democrats in Encino. Congressman Tom Rees spoke and supported the entire Democratic ticket. Butchko spoke with some people there, and he told some people that Nixon had started out way ahead in 1968, but that he lost ground when Johnson stopped all bombing of North Vietnam on October 31, 1968. This statement was followed by an increase in pro-Butchko signals in the media. Someone at this party asked who John Butchko is. Toni Kimmell said that was like asking who Tom Rees is. In about September 1972, Butchko spoke at a meeting of the Reseda-West Valley Democratic Club in Canoga Park and called for the support of the entire Democratic ticket.

Right after Butchko spoke to the Newhall Optimists, Mayor Daly of Chicago said that he was putting his Cook County machine to work for McGovern.

John Vasquez, an active Democrat in the Antelope Valley, said he saw Butchko's speech to the Sears employees in Lancaster and that Butchko gave a good speech there.

Butchko was a member of the Democratic State Central Committee of California from January 1 of 1971 until the end of 1972.

Butchko was a member of the Los Angeles County Democratic Central Committee from the time of his appointment in January of 1972 until the end of 1972.

Butchko attended as a member all of the meetings of the Los Angeles County Democratic Central Committee in 1972.

In 1972, McGovern carried the City of Los Angeles in the general election.

Throughout the day of the general election of 1972, Butchko displayed on his desk his full speech, which he had given on three occasions as a member of McGovern's Speakers Bureau. This speech was seen by many voters in surveillance on Election Day.

The most important de-escalation of the war in Vietnam was the first bombing halt of North Vietnam in 1968. The second most important de-escalation of the war in Vietnam was the second bombing halt of Vietnam in 1968.

In 1972, George Wallace was not on the ballot, where he could take votes away from Nixon.

Butchko made all the difference in de-escalating and ending the war in Vietnam.

In November, after the 1972 election, Nixon seemed to be very powerful. An article in the Los Angeles Times declared that the only question now was whether Nixon would take prisoners.

But Butchko still felt in good fettle. He was eager to continue his political activities directed toward ending United States military involvement in Indochina. He was still a member of both the Los Angeles County Democratic Central Committee, and the Democratic State Central Committee of California; his campaign of 1972, and his activities in the peace movement were still remembered by many of the politically informed people in Los Angeles County. In November of 1972, Butchko bought a new car.

Nixon seemed determined to increase his actual personal power and to suppress meaningful criticism, and he made all out efforts directed toward these objectives after the election in November and December. After the elections, there seemed to be no

196

further progress toward a settlement at the Paris negotiations. How was Nixon to be weakened? Only time would tell.

On the day before Thanksgiving, Butchko attended a meeting of the Reseda-West Valley Democratic Club at the home of Ted and Ida Lane in Canoga Park. Harold Greenberg had recently been elected president of the club, and he seemed to be interested in running for office in the West Valley. Butchko was friendly and genial at this meeting. He said that he thought it was likely that by the time of the next elections, the war in Vietnam would be ended and that new issues would become pre-eminent.

On Saturday, December 9, 1972, Butchko attended a meeting and party of the Sunland-Tujunga Democratic Club. At this meeting he was expressive. He said that the right of privacy had become an issue of major importance, and that liberals would have to struggle to obtain leadership of the Democratic Party. He said Nixon had succeeded in changing his image in 1971 and 1972 by his trips to China and Russia, which had made him look like a world statesman. When Butchko had occasion to make a statement during the formal program, he was introduced by the club president, Nancy Lund, as the California Democratic Council candidate for Congress in 1968, who had been a forthright candidate and an effective spokesman for the club's liberal views.

On December 13, 1972, Butchko attended the last meeting of the County Committee in Los Angeles for that year and exchanged greetings with Tom Carrell's former field representative and other members of the County Committee. At that meeting (or at the preceding meeting of the County Committee), Jess Unruh spoke regarding his forthcoming campaign for Mayor. Butchko listened attentively; he was sure Jess had noticed him.

197

In November of 1972, Butchko met Erwin Shaber, a leader of the Knights of Columbus on a street in Burbank. Mr. Shaber asked Butchko if he was going to run for Tom Carrell's seat. Butchko answered and replied that he did not live in Tom Carrell's district. Tom Carrell had died shortly before the general election.

On Sunday, December 17, Butchko attended a party of the Reseda-West Valley Democratic Club at the Lanes' home in Canoga Park. There was a good attendance. Butchko was confident and expressive. He said that at this time freedom of speech and the right of privacy were major issues. In those days, it was regarded as ultraliberal for a non-incumbent Democrat such as Butchko to say that the right of privacy was an issue. But Butchko knew that he had always been most effective when taking positions that were regarded as liberal by the dominant elements in politics. It then seemed as though Watergate might prove to be a thorn in Nixon's side. Nixon had called it a fantasy. Butchko had joined discussion of the issue at an early date when during all three of his major speeches for McGovern during the general election campaign, Butchko had said that McGovern believed that Nixon was behind that spying operation and that the incident demonstrated Nixon's above-the-law attitude. Butchko now called for a full investigation regarding the Watergate spying attempt.

Also at the meeting of December 17, Butchko said that the Humphrey-Muskie ticket had done better in 1968 than a Johnson-Humphrey ticket would have done, since it had gotten a larger Catholic vote than a Johnson-Humphrey ticket would have.

In December of 1972, Butchko met a member of the Young Democrats on the Golden Mall in Burbank. He told Butchko that the Young Democrats had made a secret pact to vote as a bloc for Novak at the endorsing convention for the Twenty-Seventh

Council District, regardless of what the candidates said at the endorsing convention, and that the Young Democrats had also made a pact not to tell anyone about this.

In January, Congress began an investigation of the Watergate break-in and related scandals.

Before Christmas, Nixon broke off the negotiations with North Vietnam at Paris at least temporarily and resumed heavy bombing in North Vietnam after a brief pause. From a hawk's point of view, Nixon's pre-Christmas timing for this was probably very poor.

Butchko launched a vigorous counter-propaganda program against the war policies of the Nixon Administration, by feeding into the surveillance network, which dominated politics in powerful Los Angeles County and included video surveillance in Butchko's home and office, books critical of our military involvement in Vietnam. This seemed to have some effect. On December 31, 1972, Sunday, Nixon stopped his bombing of North Vietnam, and the negotiations with the North Vietnamese at Paris were resumed early in January. Kissinger was now at the negotiations. Butchko's political activities were the major factor in bringing about the bombing halt of December 31, 1972. Also in December of 1972 Ed Davis, Otis Chandler and some others tried to make it appear that Butchko was trying to intimidate the Masons. Their attempt backfired and this contributed to bringing about the halt of the bombing in December 31, 1972.

On Thursday, January 11, Butchko attended a meeting of the Sunland-Tujunga Democratic Club. At that meeting, he said that a breakthrough in the negotiations could come at any time now, and even when it was least expected. The person to whom Butchko said this was doubtful that there would be a settlement.

199

Butchko was no longer a member of the County Committee and the Democratic State Central Committee.

But after the general election of 1972 and into 1974, many people regarded Butchko as the front runner for the Democratic nomination for Congress in the Twenty-Seventh Congressional District.

Early in January of 1973, Butchko said to his father that Otis Chandler was interfering with the peace movement by endorsing Nixon.

In January 1973, some of Butchko's opponents, including Otis Chandler, were plotting to have Butchko shot and killed. This leaked out into the surveillance network, making them look rather bad, and increasing Butchko's prestige. This made Butchko a lifelong hero. Until next Friday, Butchko's opponents were effectively silenced on a broad basis. Anti-Butchko signals in the media were silenced. Pro-Butchko signals increased. During that time the treaty ending the war in Vietnam was secretly approved and initialed.

Throughout December and January, Butchko had feeded into surveillance network statements calculated to really influential opinion behind his efforts to have the treaty signed by the end of January. On Sunday, January 21, Butchko stated for the benefit of those persons who could be reached through the surveillance network, that some of his opponents had been talking about doing to him what they talked about doing to McGovern in 1971. This seemed to silence much of his opposition through the following weekend. In other words, anti-Butchko signals were silenced. On Saturday, January 27, the treaty providing for ending United States military involvement in the war in Vietnam was officially signed. Butchko's heroism brought about the treaty ending the war in Vietnam.

Butchko attended a meeting of the Burbank Bar Association on January 29.

On February 8, he attended a meeting of the Sunland-Tujunga Democratic Club. He nominated himself for club delegate to the next annual California Democratic Council Convention to be held in Los Angeles in March. He was duly elected a delegate in the voting, which then took place.

On February 19, he attended a meeting of the Reseda-West Valley Democratic Club, and said to Ted Lane that the ending of the war in Vietnam had come as a surprise to many.

On February 15, Butchko mailed to all the newspapers in the San Fernando Valley and in the old Twenty-Seventh Congressional District and the new Twenty-Seventh District, a press release stating that he would attend the forthcoming annual convention of the California Democratic Council in Los Angeles in March. This release stated that Butchko had served as a member of the Los Angeles County Democratic Central Committee and the Democratic State Central Committee of California, and that he had won the Democratic nomination for Congress in the Twenty-Seventh Congressional District of California in 1968.

On February 20, the treaty ending United States military involvement in Laos was signed.

On February 26, Butchko attended a meeting of the Burbank Bar Association. Early in March, Butchko received a personal letter from George McGovern thanking Butchko for what McGovern aptly called Butchko's "valuable help during the campaign." Butchko' press release regarding his forthcoming attendance at the California Democratic Council Convention was published in the Record-Ledger and in the Glendale News Press. Butchko did attend the California Democratic Council Convention at the Hilton Hotel in Los Angeles on March 9, 10 and 11. Shortly after the convention the major breakthrough in discrediting Nixon occurred when Butchko fed into the surveillance network information to the effect that Nixon had engaged in the most improper surveillance activity after the general election of 1972 meaning that Nixon using Ed Davis was feeding into the surveillance network false interpretations of Butchko's actions in order to intimidate the Masons. Otis Chandler joined in this improper surveillance activity. Mr. Chandler was the publisher of the Los Angeles Times.

On March 21, Butchko attended a joint meeting of the Burbank and Glendale Bar Associations in Glendale. Baxter Ward, the newly elected Supervisor was the guest speaker. On March 28, the final withdrawal of United States military forces from South Vietnam was completed.

On April 29, Butchko attended a meeting of the San Fernando Valley Democratic Council in Tujunga. On April 30, he attended a meeting of the Burbank Bar Association.

On Saturday, May 12, he attended an important banquet of the Burbank Human Relations Council.

Before the California Democratic Council Convention in March of 1973, Butchko told some people at a meeting of the Sunland-Tujunga Democratic Club, that he was supporting Tom Bradley for Mayor of Los Angeles. This gave a big boost to Tom Bradley.

The Los Angeles Times endorsed Jesse Unruh, Tom Bradley and Tom Reddin for Mayor. Tom Bradley prevailed over all the candidates except Sam Yorty, the incumbent and went into a runoff with Sam Yorty. On the Saturday before the runoff, Butchko said in his father's house that Sam Yorty had the same wiretappers that Nixon had. Tom Bradley defeated Sam Yorty in the runoff. A reporter on KFWB said that the white vote in the San Fernando Valley did not turn out to vote for Sam Yorty. Butchko got Tom Bradley elected mayor of Los Angles in 1973.

On May 18, he attended a California Democratic Council program on the "politics of espionage" at Beverly Hills High School. Someone there said that the Watergate break in was the tip of the iceberg. On May 23, he attended an opening party of Republic Federal Savings in Burbank. On June 11, he attended another San Fernando Valley Democratic Council meeting in Studio City. On June 20, he attended a dinner meeting of the Burbank Bar Association to hear talks on the proposed City Center Redevelopment.

On June 23, he attended a party of the San Fernando Valley Fair Housing Council in Northridge. He was friendly and genial here. A black leader of the organization introduced Butchko to a group of about six people as a famous attorney and former candidate for public office.

On June 24, Butchko attended a reception for George Moscone in Woodland Hills. Butchko was genial as usual. He said to Moscone that he was looking forward to his campaign. Butchko knew that at least Moscone's campaign would tend to draw some votes from Bob Moretti, once a rival of Butchko's in the San Fernando Valley's political scene.

On June 29, Butchko attended a meeting of the Sunland-Tujunga Democratic Club at an auditorium in a local school. There was a large attendance, and Butchko asked an erudite and sharp political question of the panel.

Also on July 18, Butchko attended a meeting of the newly formed Reseda-North-West Valley Democratic Club in Encino. The Club was a merger of the Reseda-West Valley Democratic Club and the North-West Valley Democratic Club. Butchko successfully urged the Club to rejoin the San Fernando Valley Democratic Council, which it had recently left because of serious policy disagreements. Butchko was selected chairman of the by-laws committee at this meeting.

On July 19, he mailed a press release announcing his appointment to this post to about seven local newspapers.

On July 23, Butchko attended a meeting of the Burbank Bar Association. On the evening of July 23, he attended a San Fernando Valley Democratic Council meeting as a delegate representing the Sunland-Tujunga Democratic Club, and stated to the membership that he was representing the Club. He also reported on its recent activities.

On August 15, the Nixon Administration stopped all bombing in Cambodia pursuant to an Act of Congress, and all United States military intervention in Indochina came to an end.

On September 5, Butchko attended and participated in a meeting of the executive board of the Reseda North-West Valley Democratic Club. Butchko was on the executive

Board as a chairman of two committees. On September 10, he attended a meeting of the San Fernando Valley Democratic Council in Sherman Oaks.

On September 14, Butchko attended a Party honoring George McGovern and other Democrats at a home in Beverly Hills. Alan Cranston noticed Butchko's presence at this Party. Cranston introduced McGovern and promised a great deal for Democrats.

On September 15, Butchko attended a party of the Fair Housing Council of the San Fernando Valley in Van Nuys. On September 30, Butchko attended a membership meeting of the Reseda-North-West Valley Democratic Club in Northridge. On September 29, he attended a lasagna dinner and fundraising party of the Reseda-North-West Democratic Club in Woodland Hills.

On October 3, Butchko attended an executive board meeting of the Reseda-West Valley Democratic Club in Northridge; on October 11, a luncheon of the Sunland-Tujunga Democratic Club in Tujunga; on October 16, a meeting of the Board of the Burbank Human Relations Council in the Burbank Library; and on October 17, another meeting of the Reseda-North-West Valley Democratic Club. At that meeting, Ted Lane said to the full membership, during a discussion of endorsement policies that in 1972, even though he officially supported the California Democratic Council endorsed candidate for Congress in the Twenty-Seventh Congressional District as an officer of the Council, he had supported Butchko in his individual capacity. This was a favorable comment. Butchko was again vocal as he had been at so many meetings in 1973. The Club adopted its By-Laws at that meeting.

Butchko wrote and sent press releases for the various meetings of the Reseda-North-West Valley Democratic Club after his selection as publicity chairman.

Throughout 1973, as in so many preceding years, Ted and Ida Lane remained Butchko's steadfast supporters. In 1974, Ted Lane appeared on Nixon's Enemies List.

In 1973, Butchko obtained overwhelming evidence that some of the powerful surveillance crews in the Los Angeles Police Department led by Ed Davis were involved in persistent attempts to block him politically. Ed Davis fed into this surveillance network matters to intimidate the Masons so that they would not vote for Butchko.

After the general election of 1972, McGovern stated that he lost because of the Eagleton affair. McGovern carried the City of Los Angeles.

Shortly after the California Democratic Council convention in 1973, Harold Greenberg, an attorney in downtown Los Angeles, told Butchko that the Los Angles Police Department and the Glendale Police Department were supporting him (Harold Greenberg) for the Democratic nomination for Congress in the Twenty-Seventh Congressional District.

Butchko attended all the meetings and parties of the Sunland-Tujunga Democratic Club and the Reseda North-West Valley Democratic Club in 1973. On Saturday, November 10, he attended a California Democratic Council Board meeting at the Hilton Hotel in Los Angeles.

On Tuesday, December 4, 1973, at a meeting of the Sunland-Tujunga Democratic Club, he was selected to be a delegate representing the club at the forthcoming annual Convention of the California Democratic Council to be held in Sacramento in February of 1974. This was the third successive year that Butchko had been selected a Sunland-Tujunga Democratic delegate to a State Convention of the California Democratic Council.

In December, Butchko received publicity for his selection as a delegate to the convention by the Sunland-Tujunga Democratic Club in the Record Ledger and in the Glendale News-Press. The article covering this in the Record Ledger appeared on the first page of that newspaper.

In January of 1974, Butchko attended a meeting of the Sunland-Tujunga Democratic Club at which various issues positions proposed by a committee of the Club for presentation to the California State Congressional Convention were put before the Club membership. Butchko had participated actively in the work of this committee. At the Committee Butchko called for withdrawal of all non diplomatic Americans from South Vietnam and for ending aid to South Vietnam. And at the full club meeting in January, Butchko spoke briefly before the entire group in presenting some of these issues positions, including those pertaining to constitutional rights. In particular, Butchko presented a resolution that called for establishment of a permanent committee of Congress to investigate every infringement of the First Amendment Freedoms in the United States, including freedom of speech, freedom of press, freedom of association and the right of privacy.

On February 1, Butchko attended a pre-convention California Democratic Congressional meeting and party in Hollywood, where he exchanged greetings with David Roberti, Herman Sillas, Gary Davis, and Supervisor Mendelsohn of San Francisco.

Butchko attended the California Democratic Congressional Convention in Sacramento on the weekend of February 8-10, 1974. His attendance at the Convention was preceded by an article in the Tolucan of that week stating that he would attend the

California Democratic Congressional Convention as a delegate representing the Sunland-Tujunga Democratic Club.

At a meeting of the California Democratic Congressional Issues Committee, Butchko spoke briefly in favor of abolishing all filing fees in civil lawsuits during the discussion of the administration of justice.

At a caucus of delegates from the newly formed State Senate and Congressional Districts in which Butchko resided, he said that the local California Democratic Congressional Clubs should encourage those candidates who were friendly to California Democratic Congressional Council, and to the clubs, and to the people in the clubs, and should ask them to promote the clubs during their campaigns.

When Butchko returned to Burbank after the convention, he filed as a candidate for the Los Angeles County Democratic Central Committee. He was certain that some of his current opponents would go all out to defeat him. Some of the other candidates for the County Committee in his District were already friends of Butchko's.

During the first half of 1974, Butchko attended the meetings of the Sunland-Tujunga Democratic Club, the Reseda-North-West Valley Democratic Club, the Burbank Bar Association and some of the meetings of the Burbank Human Relations Council, and he continued to serve as the Publicity Chairman of the Reseda North-West Valley Democratic Club, arranging publicity for all the meetings of the club. At a meeting of the Burbank Human Relations Council on March 2, Butchko was formally introduced as a candidate for the County Committee.

At some of the meetings of the Sunland-Tujunga Democratic Club, he was introduced as a candidate for the County Committee. He also was mentioned in one of the Newsletters of the Sunland-Tujunga Democratic Club. He co-sponsored an installation dinner of the San Fernando Valley Young Democrats at the Encino Smokehouse on March 28.

But Butchko could not get elected to the County Committee in 1974. The Registrar of Voters Office had put him in the ninth place on the ballot among nine candidates in his district. All seven of the incumbents were re-elected. But Butchko received a respectable vote total of over 11,000 votes, which were more votes than the other non-incumbent candidate received.

He did this in spite of a fierce smear campaign directed by Otis Chandler and by some of his other powerful current opponents, some of whom were engaged in concerted surveillance tactics for the purpose of taking insignificant things out of context to fight dishonestly against Butchko. At various times during the campaign, some of the wiretappers and camera crews of the Los Angeles Police Department were involved in these tactics. These tactics included placing false interpretations on Butchko's mannerisms and actions in order to intimidate the Masons so that they would not vote for Butchko. The City Manager of Burbank, Joe Baker, also used these tactics against Butchko. Otis Chandler did also.

Butchko's effort to win election to the County Committee was defeated by those surveillance tactics. On Election Day someone with the Burbank police department parked a Burbank police car in Butchko's small parking lot in back of his office and left it there all day.

Butchko was under video surveillance since Nixon was elected President.

Butchko was now under complete surveillance wherever he went. He had first learned about the video surveillance in his home and office in January of 1971. The video surveillance was now in his car and also in most other places he went. Throughout 1974, some of the persons engaged in surveillance used these cameras for the attempted purpose of annoying Butchko and for the attempted purpose of distracting him from his work. The video surveillance was also used by some of the persons engaged in surveillance for the purpose of preventing Butchko from writing anything in private with a view to early publication or otherwise.

After the election in June, some of Butchko's opponents escalated their smear campaign against Butchko.

In effect, Reinecke was singled out for unusually harsh treatment by the special prosecutors of the Justice Department and in July of 1974, Reinecke was convicted of perjury in Washington, D.C., while he was still the elected Lieutenant Governor of California. Throughout 1973, Reinecke had been the front-runner in all polls for the Republican nomination for Governor of California. In all polls, Reinecke was leading each Democrat by over a million votes.

After this happened to Reinecke, some of Butchko's current opponents escalated their smear campaign against Butchko.

Throughout 1974, it was clear that they were seeking to falsely discredit Butchko and his claims to have done so much to have ended the War in Vietnam. They felt that if they could falsely discredit him now, that would destroy the credibility of his claims of having accomplished so much.

But no amount of subsequent political manipulations could effectively discredit Butchko's statements of past history.

On August 9, 1974, Nixon resigned from the Presidency in order to avoid being impeached.

The breakthrough in truthfully discrediting Nixon came in March, April and May of 1973 after Butchko fed into the surveillance network information to the effect that in 1973 Nixon using Ed Davis was involved in the most highly improper surveillance activities.

In a televised defense of himself in 1973, Nixon expressly denied that anything "improper" had originated with him. At that time, Ed Davis was Nixon's chief wiretapper for Southern California.

In June of 1974, Butchko became the first Publicity Chairman of the Twenty-Second Congressional District Democratic Council, which consisted of members of the Los Angeles County Democratic Central Committee, the Democratic State Central Committee and delegates from all the Democratic clubs in the District encompassing Burbank, Glendale, Pasadena, Sunland, Tujunga, La Crescenta, La Canada and Altadena. An article in the Record Ledger announced that Butchko had become the Publicity Chairman of the Twenty-Second Congressional District Democratic Council. As Publicity Chairman, Butchko arranged to have published in newspapers throughout the district press releases for the meetings and parties that the Council was involved in in 1974 as part of its program to coordinate the activities of its members and the Democratic clubs, and to promote the campaign of Democratic candidates in the area.

211

In the summer of 1974, Butchko became a member of Democrats United, a Democratic club in Burbank. Butchko arranged publicity in the Valley Green Sheet for a party and for a rally sponsored by this club in 1974.

At a meeting of the Sunland-Tujunga Democratic club at a church hall in Tujunga on July 24, Butchko commented, as a member of the audience in a group discussion of disarmament questions, on the importance of bringing China into disarmament negotiations.

On August 12, 1974, Butchko attended and spoke briefly at the first meeting, held in Pasadena, of the Steering Committee for the District caucus to select delegates to the Democratic Charter Conference that was held in Kansas City in December of 1974 to provide a Charter for the national Democratic Party. Butchko became a member of the Steering Committee, and on September 4, he became the Press and Publicity Chairman of the Steering Committee for the District Caucus.

Throughout 1974, Butchko attended the meetings of the Burbank Bar Association.

On January 21, 1975, Butchko was elected provisional Vice-Chairman of the Twenty-Second Congressional District Democratic Council at a meeting of the Council in Burbank. At that time, the Council was in the process of becoming the Twenty-First State Senate District Democratic Council. Butchko also became the first Chairman of the By-Laws Committee of the Council, while continuing as the Publicity Chairman. Butchko did much of the work involved in preparing the first set of By-Laws for the Council, in presenting them for approval at meetings of the By-Laws Committee in January and February and at meetings of the Council in February and March.

On February 9, Butchko spoke on the issues as part of the Sunland-Tujunga Democratic Club's group discussion of issues and resolutions for presentation to the annual convention of the California Democratic Council of 1975. On February 26, Butchko was elected a delegate to represent the Sunland-Tujunga Democratic Club at the annual convention of the California Democratic Council in Fresno on March 14, 15 and 16. At that meeting on February 26, Vince Carson presented a proposed resolution, which he said had been written by John Butchko in their Committee work. This resolution called for federal legislation to prohibit all wiretapping and all electronic surveillance in the United States, and to guarantee the right of privacy to all persons in the United States. The resolution was passed unanimously at this meeting, and it became a part of the list of resolutions, which the Club officially presented in writing to the California Democratic Committee Convention's Resolutions Committee.

On Saturday, March 1, Butchko participated in an all day meeting of the credentials Committee for the forthcoming California Democratic Council Convention at the California Democratic Council office in Los Angeles.

Butchko attended the California Democratic Council Convention in Fresno on March 14, 15 and 16. As a member of the Credentials Committee, he worked at the Credentials table on March 14. In the convention hotel, Butchko exchanged greetings with State Senator Nate Holden, the President of the California Democratic Council, and Nate said to Butchko that it was good to see him. At the convention, Paul Lewis, the former President and a leader of the Northeast Valley Democratic Club, exchanged friendly greetings with Butchko and introduced him to the new President of that Club.

213

At the convention, Vince Carson told Butchko that Butchko's resolution regarding the federal prohibition of all wiretapping and electronic surveillance passed in the convention's Resolutions Committee. However, it was mysteriously deleted from the list of resolutions, which after passing in the Resolutions Committee were then typed, mimeographed and presented for consideration on the floor of the convention.

On March 18, the Twenty-First State Senate District Democratic Council adopted its By-Laws after Butchko reported on the final changes in the By-Laws that had been made in Committee following the Council's earlier discussion of By-Laws.

After the new election of officers on March 18, 1975, Butchko was still the Publicity Chairman and a member of the Executive Board of the Council.

From January through April of 1975, Butchko attended all the meetings and parties of the Council, of the Sunland-Tujunga Democratic Club, and of Democrats United. On April 28, Butchko was elected Vice-President of Democrats United and a delegate to the Council from that club. Butchko arranged for publicity for that club's meeting and parties during most of 1975.

After Butchko was elected vice-president of Democrats United of Burbank, an article announcing that fact was published in the Glendale Ledger, the successor newspaper to the Glendale Independent. This newspaper was delivered to most residences in Glendale. This article stated that John T. Butchko has been elected vice president of Democrats United of Burbank; that Butchko is an attorney in Burbank; that he has served as a member of the Los Angeles County Democratic Central Committee and the Democratic State Central Committee of California; and that in 1968, Butchko won the Democratic nomination for Congress in the former Twenty-Seventh

214

Congressional District, encompassing large portions of the San Fernando Valley and the entire northern portion of Los Angeles County.

On May 20, 1975, Butchko attended as a delegate a meeting of the Twenty-First State Senate Democratic Council at Bob McBride's home in Pasadena. He reported on the work of the Publicity Committee, and he introduced a resolution that all Council meetings be made open to the public so that more publicity could be obtained for the meetings. This resolution passed by a vote of ten to eight.

On Saturday, May 21, Butchko attended a Legislative Conference of the American Civil Liberties Union at the University of Southern California. On the evening of Saturday, May 21, Butchko was officially installed as vice-president of Democrats United at its annual installation dinner. Donna Woodburn was installed as President of the Club. Donna was always nice to Butchko. Butchko had successfully arranged publicity for this installation dinner, and it was heavily attended.

On Monday, June 9, Butchko attended a meeting of the Executive Board of Democrats United at Donna Woodburn's home. At his meeting, Butchko suggested that the club affiliate with the California Democratic Council. On June 23, he attended a meeting of the Executive Board of the Council in Glendale. At this meeting, Dick Hallin formally resigned as Chairman of the Council, and Butchko was nominated to succeed him as Chairman of the Council.

On July 10, Butchko attended a meeting of the nominating committee of the Council at which persons were nominated for Chairpersonships of certain of the Council's Committees.

On Tuesday, July 15, 1975, Butchko was unanimously elected Chairman of the Council at a meeting at the home of Frank Trotta in Burbank. Butchko presided over the meeting following his election, and he appointed certain persons to chair committees of the Council. Butchko continued to serve as publicity Chairman of the Council. And Butchko also served as the Publicity Chairman of Democrats United of Burbank. At the meeting when Butchko was elected Chairman of the Council, the husband of a black woman, who had served as President of the Sunland-Tujunga Democratic Club and was a member of the County Democratic Central Committee said to Butchko: "You paid your dues." As chairman of the Council Butchko was in a position of power. As Chairman of the Council, Butchko had enough status to send out press releases.

The territory of the Twenty-First State Senate District Democratic Council included all the areas embraced within the Twenty-Second Congressional District and also South Pasadena. The clubs affiliated with the Council at that time were the Sunland-Tujunga Democratic Club, Democrats United of Burbank, The Glendale Democratic Forum, the Pasadena Council Club, the South Pasadena Democratic Club, and the Foothill New-Democratic Club. This Council was chartered by the Los Angeles County Democratic Central Committee.

On July 28, Butchko attended a meeting of the Burbank Bar Association.

On Monday, August 4, Butchko attended a meeting of the Executive Board of Democrats United, and successfully proposed having a regular membership meeting of the club in September in addition to the special spaghetti dinner and fund-raising party to be held September, 21.

On Friday, August 8, Butchko attended a Party in Pasadena at which Senator Tunny was the featured speaker. Before he spoke, Tunney said to Butchko, "Hello John, it's good to see you."

Later that evening, Otis Chandler began using the surveillance devices to make clicking, banging, and snapping noises for the purpose of annoying and distracting Butchko. He continued to make these noises at all hours of the day and night in Butchko's home and office and sometimes in Butchko's automobile throughout the remainder of 1975.

On Saturday, August 16, Butchko attended a fundraising party of Glendale Democratic Forum. He was introduced as Chairman of the Twenty-First State Senate District Council, and a very important man. He spoke to a good size crowd pledging that the council would try hard for Democratic successes in the months and years ahead.

When Butchko was chairman of the Council, Donna Woodburn said to Butchko that a member of the Burbank City Council wanted to ask Butchko if he (that Councilman) could run for Congress,

On August 19, Butchko wrote a letter to the Attorney General of the State of California explaining in detail how Otis Chandler was using the electronic devices to make annoying noises. Butchko said that it was an urgent situation, and he asked for an investigation by the Attorney General's Office. Butchko knew that the police could not be trusted because of, among other things, the improper and dishonest use of electronic devices by the wiretapers of the Los Angeles Police Department which had taken place so much in 1973 and 1974 and by political allies of Ed Davis in 1975.

217

On Thursday, August 21, Butchko presided over a meeting of the Executive Board of the Council at a home in Pasadena.

On August 25, Butchko attended a meeting of the Burbank Bar Association.

By Sunday, September 7, 1975, Butchko still had not received any reply from Evelle Younger's Office, and Butchko correctly concluded that Younger would do nothing to investigate the situation or to stop the noise, and that it would not be stopped. Butchko then decided to go out of politics, and he informed Donna Woodburn that he was resigning as Chairman of the Council and from his other political positions.

In 1975, a reporter on KFWB stated that the Democratic Party would not hold its 1976 convention in Los Angeles because of Ed Davis.

In 1978 when Ed Davis was running for the Republican nomination for Governor, Ed Davis said that when he was Chief of Police of Los Angeles, he twisted the tails of the liberals. Ed Davis called for United States withdrawal from the United Nations. Butchko was primarily responsible for getting the Watergate Babies elected to Congress in 1974. In 1974, Butchko got Jerry Brown elected Governor of California.

In 1976, Butchko got the Democratic nomination for Jimmy Carter over Humphrey and Jerry Brown. Butchko got Jimmy Carter elected President in 1976.

In 1984, Butchko got the Democratic nomination for President for Walter Mondale over Gary Hart by saying that Otis Chandler was supporting Gary Hart.

In 1988, Butchko got the Democratic nomination for Michael Dukakis over Richard Gephardt, by saying that Otis Chandler was supporting Gephardt.

In 1992, Butchko got the Democratic nomination for Bill Clinton over Jerry Brown by saying that Otis Chandler was supporting Jerry Brown.

In 2000, Butchko helped Al Gore get the Democratic nomination for President over Bill Bradley.

In 2004, Butchko helped John Kerry get the Democratic nomination over John Edwards.

In 2008, Butchko got the Democratic nomination for President for Barack Obama.

In 2008, Butchko got Barack Obama elected President.

In 2012, Butchko got Barack Obama re-elected President.

In 2016, Butchko got the Democratic nomination for President for Hillary Clinton. Butchko received a letter from Hillary Clinton thanking him for his support.

When Jimmy Carter was President, Butchko was the major factor in bringing about the Camp David Agreement, the peace treaty between Israel and Egypt. When Jimmy Carter was President, Butchko molded Jimmy Carter's foreign policy.

When Ronald Reagan was President, Butchko was the first prominent American who said that the United States should withdraw from Lebanon.

In about 1975, Gerald Ford and George McGovern said that Israel should negotiate with the PLO.

When Jimmy Carter was President, Israel invaded Lebanon. The Los Angeles Times, in an editorial, supported this invasion. Butchko, under surveillance, told Jimmy Carter to get Israel to withdraw from Lebanon. Then Jimmy Carter got Israel to withdraw from Lebanon.

In the 1990's, Tom Bradley signaled that Butchko was "historic". In 2013 and 2014, Butchko was a member of the Democratic National Committee. In the twentieth century, Butchko helped bring about the INF Treaty and the first START Treaty with the Soviet Union. These were disarmament treaties.

In 1938, the historian , Arnold Toynbee said that in order to prevent Western civilization from becoming a disintegrating civilization, it needed a reversion to its ancestral religion. From early 1973 through August of 1975, Butchko initiated a religious revival feeding into the surveillance network large portions of the New Testament, including Saint John's Gospel, on numerous occasions.

In 1974, Butchko fed into the surveillance network Father O'Connell's Advanced Baltimore Catechism (this was a textbook on Catholic Theology).

In 1981 through 1983, Butchko initiated a religious revival by feeding into surveillance network large portions of the New Testament, including mostly entire gospels, on numerous occasions. From January 1 through June of 1983, Butchko fed into the surveillance network an entire long gospel (St. Luke's, Saint Matthew's or Saint John's) on each day.

From 1985 through 1987, Butchko initiated a religious revival by feeding into the surveillance network large portions of the New Testament, including mostly entire gospels, on numerous occasions.

In 1995 and 1996, Butchko initiated a religious revival by feeding into the surveillance network large portions of the New Testament, on numerous occasions. On various other times in the 1990's Butchko fed into the surveillance network entire gospels.

In 2001 through 2016, Butchko initiated a religious revival by feeding into the surveillance network large portions of the New Testament usually an entire Gospel on numerous occasions.

By initiating these religious revivals, Butchko saved Western Civilization from disintegrating and brought about freedom of religion in the Soviet Union.

By initiating the religious revival in the 1970's, Butchko soundly defeated secular humanism.

By initiating religious revivals in the 1980's and 1990's, Butchko prevented secular humanism from making a comeback.

The political movement known as secular humanism was atheist, intolerant and vicious and reactionary.

In about April of 2008 Butchko introduced at a meeting of the Glendale Democratic Club a resolution stating that the club favored an immediate withdrawal of United States troops from Iraq. This resolution was passed.

When John Van de Kamp was District Attorney, Butchko wrote to him regarding the video surveillance and the noise. Van de Kemp's office said they would do nothing unless Butchko found an electronic device used for surveillance and found it in presence of a witness. This discouraged Butchko from seeking any help from the District Attorney's office. The first time that Van de Kamp ran for attorney General, the ACLU refused to endorse Van de Kamp in the Democratic primary, on the grounds that as District Attorney, Van de Kamp did not prosecute police shootings.

In the 1974 edition of the Legal Directory published by Martindale Hubbell, the leading national directory, the authors of that directory gave Butchko a Bv rating. That rating meant good and very highly recommended. In those days, most attorneys were not rated.

A biographical sketch of Butchko was published in "Who's Who in American politics" published by a firm in Arizona in their Second, Third, and Fourth Editions for the years 1969-1970; 1971-1972 and 1973-1974, respectively. In the late 1970's the Burbank Area History was published. Butchko's resume' occupied a position in that book.

When Jerry Brown was Attorney General and afterwards when Jerry Brown was Governor, Butchko wrote to Jerry Brown and asked to get the video surveillance stopped. Jerry Brown did not reply to Butchko's letters.

In the 1990's some person claimed that Butchko's articles in the Los Angeles Times San Fernando Valley section only, throughout 1968, were published only in Burbank. If that were correct, it would not alter any conclusions in this book

In the 20th century, Butchko was the major factor in bringing about the INF disarmament treaty. Also Butchko was the major factor in bringing about the first START disarmament treaty Gorbachev was watching Butchko.

It was hard to bring about these treaties because Gorbachev and the Russians were vehementy opposed to the Star Wars program of the United States.

www.ingramcontent.com/pod-product-compliance
Lightning Source LLC
Chambersburg PA
CBHW060611290526
45790CB00011B/1466